My name is Rachael Treasure. I am Australia's number one bestselling fiction author and I submit this letter as one of support for my healer and teacher, Katherine Bright and her manuscript, Connection - Keep Your Light Burning Bright.

My latest novel, The Farmer's Wife sold almost 8000 paperback copies in its first three days of release and entered at number one position as an ebook for HarperCollins Australia. The Farmer's Wife will be sold into the United States market in July 2013 and will be published alongside my other four novels in both Germany and the United Kingdom.

The reason I so passionately support Katherine and her manuscript is I know her work needs to be published and shared with the world. She has made all the difference in my personal and professional life. With her help, I have been able to grow as a human being and author so I can weave the message of lightwork and healing into my novels for readers of popular fiction.

It was Katherine who inspired the character of Evie in my last two novels, and the overwhelming feedback from readers about the spiritual messages in the book has been confirmation that it is now time for Katherine's teachings to reach a wider readership.

I keep two books next to my bed at all times as a guide for my life and inspiration for my writing. One is Ask and It is Given by Esther and Jerry Hicks, the other is You Can Heal Your Life by Louise Hay but I believe a third very special book needs to be added to that collection. That book is Katherine's, Connection—Keep Your Light Burning Bright.

I have read Katherine Bright's insightful, entertaining and practical book and know it is one that would become a well-loved reference book to be used over and over by thousands of people on this planet. I wish you well and thank you for your time,

Rachael Treasure
Australia's Best Selling Author
05 May 2013

TESTIMONIAL/ENDORSEMENT

The basis of Katherine's uniqueness is her Humanity. From the first, there is delight in her being approachable, natural, light-hearted & grounded—she creates an immediate sense of fraternity & affinity, whether in a group or one to one situation. She relates as an equal, sharing the commonalities as a soul living an everyday human life—she touches the soul. This creates the space of comfort, ease and trust in which openness can occur & Lightness flow.

Her teaching and healing carries the absolute energy of Authenticity and Integrity. And the delightful thing is, this gift can be wrapped in down-to-earth laughter and fun-loving manner; gentle guiding; profound focus; or compassionate tenderness—it resonates unfailingly with what we know to be our highest truths.

Overriding all is the obvious breadth and depth of her own Enlightenment. Katherine's dedication, commitment, vision and knowlege are evident to all who meet her, creating the recognition of spiritual mastership and the inspiration to follow the heart's opening. But no mistake, as in all truly Enlightened, the grace of humility is at the centre of the gift . . .

Anne Boxsell, *Bruny Island Tasmania 2012*

Katherine's book Connection—Keep Your Light Burning Bright was a revelation to me when I first read it in connection with a foundational workshop I was doing with her at the time. Since then I have gone on to do other workshops and personal mentoring with Katherine in order to build my skills and knowledge for working with Creator in my personal and professional life. I regularly return to read this foundational book to refresh my knowledge and understanding, especially when I am learning new things. This is the same approach that I have used in my professional work as an educator for close to twenty years. I consistently return to the foundations in order to reconstruct my knowledge and provide a reinforcing base for the new. I hope that you find this book as important in your personal and professional life as I do!

Kathryn Meldrum PhD
Co-author of Learning to Teach Health and Physical Education
May 2013

Consultations / Healings

"I first spoke to Katherine in 2005 the week after my mum died. A friend had told us about her and booked a phone consultation for Mum the week before, and we had booked a second one. However, when Mum passed away, my sister and I decided that I should keep the appointment. At the time, I was feeling most of the usual symptoms of grief as well as a bunch of other quite negative emotions. I was already a healer myself, but nothing I was doing was helping. It was definitely one of the lowest points in my life. So I rang Katherine thinking, *What have I got to lose?* That phone call is still one of the best things I've done in my life. Forty-five minutes later, I was a new person. There was still grief, but I was myself again and I could deal with it. I can't remember much about the conversation, but I know it worked and that's what mattered. Since then I have done a heap of Katherine's courses and forums as well as a trip to Peru. All have been extremely worthwhile and many have been fabulous. I have met wonderful people, and we have done great work together. I believe Katherine does very important work, and I can't thank her enough for how she has helped me. I am glad though that with the techniques I have learnt from her I have been able to help her at times in return as well as others and the planet."

Karina Noontil, *Secondary Teacher and Healer, November 2009*

"I would honestly have to say the amount of shifts that I have had in my life since I started seeing Katherine have been phenomenal. I have got that much more confidence in myself and have cleared massive amounts of old stuff that I don't feel I have to deal with anymore. I had a medical condition and have seen two separate doctors, both of which have said that my condition has now completely resolved after medical test results returned. I am blown away by that because it is medically proven."

Brody Cummings, *Hobart, 2006*

"Thank you for all your work, information, and techniques that you've given me to enlighten life's purpose and healing."

Debbie Penney, *Cairns, 2006*

"Thank you for everything during this year . . . your work and you are much appreciated!"

Jan Hecksher, *Melbourne, 2008*

"As per our phone healing today, I would like to tell you what has happened for me since The Creator rewired my brain and cured my dyslexia. While I still have problems with some spelling of words, I have noticed that I have been seeing colours in a different way than I was used to seeing and experiencing them. As you know, I am quite proud of my garden, and when I look at the flowers, their colours are exquisite. I have never seen the colours as that vibrant before the rewiring. My whole experience of the world is so new that I find myself continually amazed at the colours of everything around me. Life is so much more colourful."

Sid Bintley, *aged in his seventies, Tasmania, 2007*

"I have Multiple Sclerosis and have had healing sessions with Katherine on multiple occasions. Katherine has worked on my spine and taken my lumbar pain levels from nine out of ten to a zero out of ten levels within one session. This is wonderful and really worthwhile to help me manage. With Creator she has also dissolved bladder and kidney stones."

John Giannopoulos, *Melbourne, 2008*

"I have attended a few of Katherine's courses and have loved every one of them. Katherine brings a real element of fun and lightness to her work, which makes the experience not only fulfilling but easy-going too. Having not had much experience in personal healing before, I found Katherine's methods helped me to relax and trust my own abilities without my head getting in the way. She has helped me develop skills that I never knew I had, or never thought I could have—I can't tell you what a thrill that is for me! I can clear my own issues in an instant and help others around me to do the same. What a joy! Katherine also keeps herself on the same level as everyone else so while you are amazed by her skills, it doesn't make you feel inferior or lacking in any way. I always feel safe, loved, and very, very happy when I do her work. As I work within the corporate world, I am so grateful to have these tools to manage the stress and negativity I face on a daily basis and instead create a peaceful loving life for myself and those around me. It has really made the most extraordinary difference to my life, and I am forever grateful."

Yolande Abeling, *Telecommunications Executive, 2007*

"This was a very enlightening course for me. I discovered interesting aspects about myself. Now the basics are known, I use this technique almost daily for all kinds of things. Even at work! Kathy teaches on high standards in integrity making the atmosphere feel very safe and comfortable. Thank you for your visit in The Netherlands."

Mark van der Putten, *Helmond, The Netherlands, November 2009*

"There are no words for an experience like that; it's a present!"

Angelique Fierens, *Helmond, The Netherlands, November 2009*

"In April this year (2009), Katherine paid a visit to Holland, and we had the opportunity to benefit from her expertise and guidance during her stay. Katherine is a wonderful person with a great sense of humor, who has the ability to make you feel comfortable in any situation and so you feel free to 'open up' to any experience she may guide you through. I attended several of Katherine's classes, and every single one of them has been a treat. Whether I look back on the very intense Reiki 2 class or the eye-opening connecting to the creator or the astonishing communicating with crystals, which was such a wonderful experience, that I completely fell in love with them and find myself trying to communicate with every crystal I can lay my hands on. Katherine teaches her classes and shares her knowledge and believes with great expertise and a sound sense of humor; there wasn't a dull moment. She makes you aware of yourself and your abilities and encourages you to explore them. She brought peace and relief to my heart and soul, a big smile on my face and she surely widened my horizon."

Ellen van der Putten, *Helmond, The Netherlands, November 2009*

"Working with Katherine was a very positive and impressive experience. Due to her natural and open way of speaking, she is able to guide you through your own mind and body. This experience had a healing effect and made me a better person. As well as physical as mental meaning. I hope to meet Katherine in the future and to learn a lot more about myself with her as guide."

Frans Mouws, *Dutch author and filmmaker, Helmond, The Netherlands, November 2009*

"I've learned different healing techniques from Katherine. Her commitment and positive energy made these learnings extra special for me. At her last visit to the Netherlands, she aligned me to use the Reiki II symbols. These techniques helped me to expand the usage of healing. I'm very grateful for this."

Bas van der Putten, *Helmond, The Netherlands, November 2009*

"I would like to encourage all health professionals to explore Katherine's work. Her compassion and empathy allowed me to discover many new dimensions to helping and healing others. Every patient now has a silver lining with thanks to Katherine. I am now a more patient and understanding person and veterinarian. I more easily find a point of stillness in my work."

Dr Susan Peden, *Veterinarian BVSc (Hons) MACVS (small animal surgery), 2007*

"Awesome!"

Tania Bennett, *Perth, WA 2006*

"I can highly recommend the teachings as presented by Katherine. She presents in a clear, authoritative way with no pretensions. She makes everyone feel loved and cared for all during the course. Meanwhile, Katherine continues to be a prime example of the efficacy of what she teaches, performing little miracles all the way through in such a natural and easy-going way. She gently urges us all on, into the mystery of this truly magnificent healing work, and by the time we're done; we begin to feel like masters too! Well done, Master Katherine!"

Mas Rogers, *founder of "Heart Radiance," Melbourne, 2006*

"Thank you for your exquisite workshop, Accessing Interdimensional Portals and Paths."

Hans-Christian Kleist, *Eumundi, Qld, 2007*

"You have completely changed my flat life into a multicoloured flying balloon. With gratitude eternally."

Carol Mahannah, *Canada, 2005*

"I just wanted to say thank you to you again. Those four days have had a huge impact on my life, that I'll always be grateful to you. I am looking forward to level 2 and 3. God Bless."

Julie Pearce, *Brisbane, 2006*

"Eight years ago, I was diagnosed with having emphysema. My breathing had been restricted, until I recently attended a healing workshop facilitated by Katherine. With the release of trauma, fear, and negative beliefs from my body, I am delighted to discover that I am breathing with ease once again. This has been a life-changing experience for me. I look to the future with excitement and joy. Many thanks to Katherine for sharing her knowledge with wisdom, truth and vision. She created a space in which I felt both safe and comfortable. Her level of energy was contagious, and I enjoyed myself immensely. Katherine's ability to teach is outstanding, her wealth of knowledge is vast and highly valued, and I learnt in a fun environment with an out-standing group of people. As a result, I believe I have been greatly enriched by the experience. God Bless."

Lesley Martin, *Melbourne, 2006*

"I feel I need to share this with you. Before hearing about you, I had been very blessed to often hear the Angels sing anytime and to hear native American Indian music also mainly when meditating, so to hear the Angels music come from *you* has been truly amazing! When explaining what I would hear to my husband, I could find nothing on earth to compare it to and well now I do! Thanks heaps . . . I am still absorbing all that I experienced at your seminar and feel truly blessed to have been a part of it. You are a wonderful woman with an amazing gift, and I will always be grateful for you sharing this with me and the rest of the group."

Annette Plumridge, *Melbourne, 2007*

"A life-changing experience—thank you from the inner essence of my being . . . I salute you. With love."

Jill Ness, *Melbourne, 2005*

"Thank you for showing me the way to have light and love in my life."

Melanie Boon, *Port Douglas, Qld, 2006*

"I so enjoyed your course in Port Douglas, and please let me know about the next stage!"

Pamela Martin, *Daintree, Qld, 2006*

"After completing the level 1 course, Management of Your Connection to God—Connection to the Universal Heart, I found myself wanting to understand more about the inner healing qualities we all possess and was fortunate to have the opportunity to undertake the 'Chromosomal Disorders' course. This course enabled me, and everyone else, to connect with the Creator and do some amazing healings. These two courses have helped make everything in my life so much clearer. Katherine is a wonderful teacher and a great inspiration to us all. I would not have been able to channel the energy of the Creator or understand the wealth of energy inside me without her caring nature and gifted guidance. Thanks, Katherine, you have made a wonderful and lasting impact on my life."

Kathryn Fox, *Tasmania, 2009*

"I attended my Reiki 1 Certificate course with mixed emotions, I must admit. I was nervous and slightly apprehensive as I had been seeking a spiritual and healing modality to add to my clinical hypnotherapy training. It was very important to me that I was able to 'feel' some type of energy in order for me to add Reiki to my work in good faith. Within moments of listening to Katherine speak, I knew I was in the right place. Before me sat a woman of wisdom, grace, and beautiful energy all blended perfectly with a down-to-earth and fun-loving approach to life, love, and Creator. I felt as if I had come home. Katherine vocalizes the soul's inherent wisdom, and that truth harmonizes with every chord in the heart and spirit. Katherine is a wonderful teacher, intuitive, insightful, and warm, a true link to Creator, and a powerful instrument of his healing work on earth. I can now add Reiki to my work without hesitation, knowing that I have been taught by a true master. If you are thinking of learning Reiki, or attending any of Katherine's courses or seminars, I urge you with all my heart, to do your Soul the favour."

Jasmine Wylder, *Dip.cln.Hyp, IED Practitioner, Hobart, 2007*

"Stereotypes of farmers show us to be a very narrow minded lot. Not the rural folk in this district though. Yes we have 'old fashioned' values—but there's a new movement here, thanks to one woman . . . Katherine Bright. Kathy is a normal suburban mum living in Sorell, but she has the gift of healing. And that's no bull. She's helped everyone from shearers with chronically bad backs to busy farm mums who can't quite get back in the saddle after having children, and wee babies with drastic illnesses. Not only that, she's taught many of us about spirituality and healing, and she's opened up a whole new world for the Bundy Girls like me in this district. Before I met Kathy, spirituality was merely about man-made churches and boring services that I had to sit through for school. Now there's a load of us up this way with a new spin on God, medical problems and healing. Thanks to Kathy the girls round here have used Reiki on sheep, horses and the odd chook! She's been so inspirational to our district; I plan to base a character on her for my next novel, *The Cattlemen*. The concepts she teaches make a whole lot of sense to us who work with animals and the land . . . In her words, 'Because we are less able to differentiate between that of a natural and man-made frequency due our desensitization in modern society and cities we may not understand many of God's natural and automatic laws and prescriptions. We do not really understand the changes of the seasons any more nor the electrical fields of the trees unless we spend time with nature; unless we live away from these electromagnetic fields and radiation devices. Most of us have lost the ability to converse, understand and sense the actions of natural beings like the animals and birds.' Take a look at her website . . . www.katherinebrightaustralia.com."

Rachael Treasure 2008, www.rachaeltreasure.com

"Last week's book launch in Hobart was a great chance to thank all the people who have helped me on my journey! Here's a great mate, Katherine Bright, who I met several years ago when I needed Bowen Therapy for my very sore back that had endured hours at the computer, farm work and pregnancy! She's sorted many a shearer's aches and pains. Since then, Katherine has become a remarkable teacher for me. She helped me develop the character of Evie in *The Cattleman's Daughter* and has been a fantastic support to me and my children. She's also a busy mum who works from home with her business Lightworkers International."

Rachael Treasure, Penguin books, One of their top three best-selling authors, 2009
(excerpt taken from www.rachaeltreasure.com on November 5, 2009)

"*A big thank-you* for a wonderful week spent with you and my kind of normal people . . . was just the *best*! I had a lot of fun into the bargain. I put both bottles of your Light Frequency Essences that I bought from you into the Tully River—a few kilometres above where the farming starts and a km or so below where the Hydro Power Station is in order to assist the healing of the waterway. It is so beautiful up there. Thanks again for all the wonderful work you do for us all and the planet."

Bev Haack, *Cairns, Qld, 2009*

"Attending the Accessing Patterned and Hereditary Chromosomal Disorders class in January 2009, I have felt totally relaxed and comfortable to be myself, totally free and with so much joy. The class was amazing! I learned a whole new perspective about how this work affects the whole package of the self, body systems, emotional, spiritual and mental energetics, etc. It was like three years of a naturopathy course in 6 days, but delivered in such a way that that wasn't difficult. Katherine is amazingly grounded and in tune as a teacher. She is multidimensional and such a light worker!"

Heather Coburn, *Hobart, 2009*

"Hi, Katherine, Just thought I'd let you know I did have fun on the course! It was such a wonderful experience. I'm still processing the alterations and information, but I did want to let you know that the biggest change has been with my horse. After connecting to his higher self and feeling how terrified of the ostriches and emus he actually is, I did as you suggested and asked creator to download information to him on how to help him cope and understand the issues and to know he was safe. My partnership with him has altered so much that when my friend and I went for a ride today (Sunday) he calmly walked past the ostriches and emus. You wouldn't believe how impressed my friend was. Her jaw was on the ground! It was such an amazing experience as last week end I very nearly came off him due to the ostriches and emus doing exactly the same thing as they did today! What an amazing difference! To know that he trusts me and can overcome such a huge fear with the simple connection I had with him is awesome! Thank you so much for allowing me to learn these life-altering skills! I look forward to using them more and to furthering these skills with the next level! Again, Thanks so much. Light and love!"

Tania Bailey, *Tasmania, July 09*

"A simple thank-you just doesn't seem anywhere near enough to say to a person who has saved your life on so many occasions. You have helped me to understand who I am and given me the tools to have a relationship with Creator, which has changed my world and made it a beautiful place to call home. May you always have an abundance of love and light in your life, as I think you are an amazing and valuable human being. Love and blessings."

Tina Williams, *Hobart, Tasmania, 2011*

"I am so grateful for Katherine Bright. I had never known that healing could be so gentle and nurturing until I started talking to Katherine. Katherine has helped me move forward in areas that I felt stuck in for a long time and I feel so happy to tell the world about what she does as I truly believe in her and her work. Thank you, Katherine, for spreading the light."

Kristianna Michaelides, *Melbourne, Sept 2012*

"Dear Katherine, I am writing to thank you for helping me with my yearlong battle with my son's eczema. We have not had clear skin almost ever, and I have been literally hitting a wall with doctors telling me it's an incurable disease which he needs to grow out of. You have been *amazing* in identifying specific foods he is reacting to and most surprisingly the dogs! Since first consulting with you, we had two weeks of absolutely clear skin with no flare ups! Without your help and insight, my son would still be suffering with extreme reactions and I wouldn't know how to help him. I am so grateful for your special gift and also your friendly and approachable manner. I hope others avail themselves of this incredibly powerful and insightful healing technique."

Alina Kleiman, *Melbourne, Sept 11*

"Nine years ago, I was infected with a tick-borne disease called Rickettsia and I developed chronic fatigue syndrome and fibromyalgia as a result of the disease going undetected and untreated for two years. For the last six years I was bed-bound, unable to walk at all and extremely low in energy. Six years of not walking do not exactly leave one with strong muscles and joints, but Katherine's healings have really helped to put my body in healing and strengthening mode rather than weak and painful mode, which has allowed me to progress quite quickly. I am now beginning to walk again; my body is getting stronger, and my energy and stamina have improved significantly. My family, friends, and doctors are amazed and delighted with my progress and the best part is that I continue to improve every week. Katherine's spiritual and energetic healings, as well as being instrumental in my healing process, are also a lot of fun! Katherine has a wonderful sense of humour, and when combined with Creator's, you can't help but rejoice in the letting go of old wounds and in opening up to everything positive that is available to us on this planet. When my illness was at its worst, I could not see a way out nor imagine a future that didn't include the many limitations I was then experiencing. Thanks to Creator and to the healing sessions I have been able to share with Katherine, so far I have been guided out of illness and limitation and into a space of healing, growth, and joy. I feel like I have reconnected to the present, and now when I look to the future, I see only brightness and endless possibility. Thank you, Katherine."

Omar Moustafa, *Melbourne, 2012*

"My eleven-year-old son was developing quite bad scoliosis. After only a few treatments with Katherine, his back is straight and he has had no pain. She was able to inform me of reasons for his problem (for example, he has been ten pin bowling since early childhood and never had any correction to his postural problem, which had developed due to muscular strain and the weight of the ball). It was simple but effective treatment. I would thoroughly recommend Bowen Therapy to anyone with any kind of back problems."

Kylie Sherwood, *Port Macquarie, NSW, April 2012*

"I have seen Katherine Bright three times now for Bowen Therapy treatment and once for naturopathic consultation. She has really helped me. I have a lot of relief from the long-term lower back, neck, and shoulder pain caused by a stressful job. I have previously had chiropractic and physiotherapy treatment that hasn't helped."

Sue Marsh, *Port Macquarie, NSW, May 2012*

Abundance Workshop:

"The abundance workshop was amazing. With Katherine's help, I was able to find 89 core belief systems in myself, such as 'I am weak' (positive) and 'I love myself' (negative) all of which we were able to clear and heal in just one day! In the process, hundreds of other belief systems blocking my abundance also got cleared. Through muscle testing, I was able to see what I really thought of myself on a subconscious level. There were countless unhelpful belief systems accumulated from past lives and genetic inheritance. Katherine showed us how to hand it all over to

Creator and trust the healing process, without which it would be virtually impossible to eradicate so many blockages at once. Many thanks for a life-changing workshop!"

Angeline Meloche, July 2012

"Thank you so much for being part of my life for the past two years. Through doing your workshops and having healings with both of you, I now have the tools to enable me to live life instead of just getting through each day. My eyes and heart are now open to the wonders of the universe, and I can truly look forward to whatever life holds for me with peace, joy, and loads of love in my heart. What a gift you have given me. Thank you for all you do to make the world a better place to be."

Jane, Bundaberg, Qld 2012

"Katherine has helped me put my life back together again. Her courses reinforce everything I need to understand and believe in who I really am. They are a continuing life learning experience."

Patricia Berry, Lindisfarne, Tasmania, 2011

"My life without your workshops and advice would be totally different. I wouldn't be where I am now without the guidance I have received. I have a direct connection with Creator now. Having this makes my life so much easier and so much smoother. My journey is being fulfilled. It is so beautiful to see love and rainbows every day no matter what I do."

Kathryn Fox, Port Macquarie, January 2013

Light-Frequency Essences
(available on www.katherinebrightaustralia.com)

Creator quoted this recommendation because Creator dictated all the recipes and the process by which these are brewed. "These essences are each lovingly hand made by Katherine. They *hold the words in the water molecules.*"

They may be used in a similar way to homeopathics. These are homeopathic-like, vibrational essences designed to strengthen and hold the energy in the water molecules of the body in order to create balance and harmony. They are healings in themselves and capable of clearing the genetic body of any blockages that are hampering understanding of the true meanings of the words they embody.

They can be used by anyone and are suitable for children and animals. Please choose to use them when drawn to them. They are subtle in fragrance but very powerful and unlock blockage held in the physical/genetic body, progressing to a spiritual clearance of blocked energy patterns, accessing even the soul levels of self. When sprayed onto the wrist and held for five seconds, each essence is transported into the water molecules of the body promoting a 'cellular understanding' of the true meaning of the 'word' title of each essence, e.g. empowerment or love. Creator's truth and sense of each become one with your cells' understanding, and disease related to the issue literally dissipates, resonating in the cells with the new meanings. This hastens clearance of emotional, spiritual, and physical disease."

"I have a nine-month-old baby, and after two very difficult months of her not sleeping well at all, I decided to use the security essence in her bath. That night, she slept through from 7:00 p.m. to 6:00 a.m. for the first time ever! She did the following night as well, and since then, while she does wake up on the odd occasion, we have noticed a significant difference in her ability to re-settle herself, and all of our sleep has benefited as a result."

Yolande Abeling, *Melbourne, 2011*

"I run a tropical fish hatchery in Tasmania! 'Love' essence is sprayed into our storage tanks. We have found a definite increase in our fertility rates since we started using this essence, which we continue to do."

Louise Willis, *2007*

"They're just yummy. Sometimes they have a subtle fragrance, and other times they don't. They seem to adjust themselves to your needs."

Brody Cummings, *2006*

"As a holistic veterinarian, I have been using these essences with both animals and their owners to help heal and support where required. I have found them very helpful and very supportive. They create a loving energy in an otherwise frantic and stressed work environment. I particularly value their use in situations where the owners are also aware of and using the essences."

Susan Peden, *Veterinarian BVSc (Hons) MACVS (small animal surgery), 2007*

"**Joy Essence:** My favourite essence—if I could even pick one—is the joy essence. It's like a little bottle of sunshine. I first started using it when I had a bad case of acne and Katherine advised me to spray some of it on my face. Well, the acne didn't last long, and neither did the accompanying feelings of sadness and self-pity. Since finding Katherine and using these wonderful essences, I have never felt so good or laughed so much in my entire life!"

Angeline Meloche, *2012*

"These essences are really good for grounding, clearing, and healing your processes when you are trying to work through issues. Katherine brews these by hand and makes special attention that each batch is updated to the new age as we progress on this journey of our planet. The new essences often have natural fragrances and adapt to you personally. I use them as room sprays as well, for cleansing and healing myself. They are really good for clearing up spaces for example before and after meetings and events. I use eternity to clear negativity and enlightenment to clean my crystals. The new peace essence is so grounding and makes you feel calm. They are really good to use before you go to sleep because they get rid of all the negative build-up of the day and you have a really peaceful sleep. Serenity and security work well for this also. I use the essences in my office to improve the mood. My baby grandson loves them and wants you to spray them on his hand. He gets a twinkle in his eye when you spray them. I use all twelve of them at different times depending on how I feel and what I need and what is going on in my life. They are very supportive like a homeopathic remedy. I highly, highly recommend them!"

Kathryn Fox, *Port Macquarie, January 2013*

Connection:
KEEP YOUR LIGHT
BURNING BRIGHT

KATHERINE F. BRIGHT, ND

BALBOA.
PRESS
A DIVISION OF HAY HOUSE

Balboa Press books may be ordered through booksellers or by contacting:

Balboa Press
A Division of Hay House
1663 Liberty Drive
Bloomington, IN 47403
www.balboapress.com.au
1-(877) 407-4847

ISBN: 978-1-4525-0997-6 (sc)
ISBN: 978-1-4525-0998-3 (e)

Printed in the United States of America

Balboa Press rev. date: 05/20/2013

DEDICATION

To my dear heart, Kim; my treasured children, Sara, Robert, Kim, and Isaac; and my special friends who have given me the love and light to be on this journey. A special thanks to creator and the beings of light. Gratitude to my special soul companions, Archangel Michael, Lord Sananda, and Mother Mary, who have sustained my beingness in all the personal ways love can be with me. Peace and grace, my heart.

www.katherinebrightaustralia.com

CONTENTS

INTRODUCTION TO THE AUTHOR

When I considered writing this book, my aim was to provide an easy and simple format for people, a way for people to realize that they are able to connect to the creative force automatically as their innate right. I wanted to tell them that this is not a difficult adventure requiring reams of information, huge volumes of study, nor is it achievable only by those who go without, struggle to attain, or remove themselves from normal life. Like most people out there on this planet, I am a family member. I am a mother of four gorgeous children. I also currently have four grandchildren. I have a loving husband. I have been divorced and endured trauma. I am, in fact, quite extraordinarily normal though I find myself completely different to the mainstream at the same time.

I live in intermingled worlds—being a soccer mum, making school runs and assisting younger and older children and a married child with her own family, and speaking with God or Creator, whichever you prefer, multiple hours per day, just existing in my every day. It didn't always start out looking that way though; like everyone else's, my life has been a journey . . . not always a pleasant one, but one which I have found to be valuable because it has grown me to be the person I am today—someone I am proud of. Would you like to feel automatically that you are proud of yourself and your journey? Even if it hasn't always looked like the fairy-tale life we assume esoterically gifted people must possess to achieve a great connection to themselves and the higher realms of spirituality?

I have endured great suffering in my life, but I have also learned how to survive and not only conquer over that phase of my life this time around but also to embrace the difficulties in a space of complete trust in the universal plan. I trust in the Creator of things bigger than myself. I speak daily with creation, and I never get "a bum steer" in the replies I receive, which guide me every day. I trust and have abundance in every way and choice. This is my life.

You may think people become zealot-like when they have connection to God or spirituality and must separate themselves in order to attain higher learning. I disagree. I think the biggest "grounders" in our existence are our families and our everyday worlds . . . no matter what that appears like to us or anyone else. From our everyday existence come the lessons of life, the perfection that can only come from working through discord successfully. The joy of a small child's smile can counteract the fatigue of lack of sleep. These things bring us a sense of satisfaction, especially when we achieve or overcome something we found challenging. From these everyday lessons, we receive great enlightenment. As an enlightened master once said, "Before enlightenment chopping wood and carting water, after enlightenment chopping wood and carting water." I add that with some more grace and ease, we may enjoy the process for its own sake.

Never deny who you are, even if another does not give it credence, because you are an individual of great grace and wisdom, just waiting to be connected to that which created you.

Please come on the journey with me and see how you experience your own connection. This book is for anyone wanting a great insight into that space. I travel worldwide doing Earth healing, spreading light, and now providing workshops to follow on from this book. So, if you want to meet up with me and experience this personally, please feel free to email me and look at my website www.katherinebrightaustralia.com. I will make contact with you or your group so you may experience the wonders of connection first-hand or just add to your current experience of spiritual practice.

Love and light, joy and abundant thought,

Katherine F. Bright (ND)

HISTORY

I have lived in Australia all my life, mostly in Tasmania, although when I was in my early twenties, I spent just over four years in Queensland, where my first child was born.

I am the younger of two children born to a Dutch migrant family, who came to Australia in the early 1950s. As with most early European migrant families, my upbringing was one of getting on with it—fitting in but being separate because my family ate a bit differently, looking like a local but not always feeling like one, and having different values sometimes—but I was also very grateful for the land on which I stood. My family worked hard to get a life together from having nothing on arrival in Australia. This is a story that all migrant families will understand.

I attended a Catholic school from prep to grade 10 and then attended a public matriculation college for years 11 and 12. I married young, and my marriage ended some time later; there followed different relationships, children, study, and journeys to get me to where I am today.

I have diplomas in naturopathy as well as in Bowen therapy and remedial massage, and I am also a qualified practicing Reiki teacher and master. I have studied many health modalities over the years, including reflexology and iridology. I commenced my spiritual journey in my childhood but have studied many different forms since then, in the way that the curious do!

I have worked professionally in the alternative health field since 1986, although sixteen years in the Australian Public Service was an enormous journey before that. That time provided me with valuable tools in learning clerical skills and understanding politics from many angles (not all of which felt comfortable). It gave me much experience in areas of employment bureaus and workers compensation, occupational health and safety policy in the workplace, customer service, book work, touch typing, and reception. I did everything from interviewing people, compiling submissions, interacting with various government officials, and editing career manuals to making the coffee and getting fed up!

Even though I enjoyed different duties and workplaces during this time and was skilled and competent in the majority, I always found myself to be the proverbial round peg in a square hole. Upon completion of my time with the public service agency, I later worked in a few temporary jobs in retail and did a little of this and a little of that before setting up my own health practice. Music is another of my passions. I have been a professional musician and vocalist and have composed musical pieces and performed them on stage. I have even produced CDs. I continue to perform as a musican and vocalist and also carry this into my current work, often performing "soul-songs" to support and enlarge the energy of the group at workshops.

I have worked now in some form of alternative health practice for twenty-eight years, and since 1992, it has been in my own clinic, which is phenomenally busy. I love it. I have a private practice in which I treat people using different methods depending on their need. I am a Bowen therapist who treats structural conditions and a naturopath looking at holistic health. My forte and absolute love in addition to these modalities is spiritual and energetic healing, teaching, and counselling. I treat people onsite and also provide telephone or Skype consultation service with clients worldwide.

In 2006, I developed the modality "Theta Resonance at All Levels," based upon my whole life's growing understanding of connection with spirit, frequency, vibration, colour, meditation, toning, and communication with Creator. I developed and formatted many courses, which have been successfully taught, including medical intuitive work involving chromosomal disorders.

From March 2010, I commenced a remodelled version of this modality. It was remodelled because—as it should be in everything esoteric—the energy needs to be current, fresh, and exciting. Connection is always that. As Creator shows me new things, I want to deliver them to you and use these tools and skills immediately. So I am dedicated to updating my work and providing the latest of my own channellings for you to enjoy and experience. I now do one-on-one counselling and mentoring with select individuals instead of large classes. I find these smaller sessions to be very satisfying. They are tailored to the individual's need and progress. One of the great joys for my network of students is get-togethers. I name them "working parties"; we heal and intend for the greater good of the planet and universal peace.

Creator asked me to write this book, and, consequently, here it is. Those of my students who have studied with me for many years will tell you that I don't let the dust settle too easily. My channel with Creator/Source is instant, accurate, direct, and based on integrity. I love Creator and the beings of light and love, and I play in that realm with such peace and joy daily. I am dedicated to establishing a way of delivering to you the empowerment to establish your own connection to Creator. It is easy, and it shouldn't be mistaken as difficult. Come enjoy and learn how truly connected we all are. We are not trying to attain new connection, really. We are always connected; the illusion of separation we have created can just get in the way of realizing this. We are all part of the universal one.

THE LAWS OF ABUNDANCE

There are already tomes written about abundance and the ways in which it can be provided to each and every one of us upon this planet. It is understood how the laws of attraction facilitate our beliefs and create our environments, realities, repercussions in some ways, and general well-being.

I want to place a difference slant on this.

Creator told me to let you know, first and foremost, that each and every one of you is different and therefore the way in which you think and attract to yourselves will be particular to you. The laws may remain constant in quantum physics, but the way in which you employ them is completely individual.

We are beings of physics. We exist as a well-ordered chaos of molecular and atomic energy capable of very individual reactions. We are souls and genetics; we are history and conditioning. We believe differently and are racially different. Therefore, how can anyone tell us the formula for our personal and individual existence?

Well, considering that Source created that existence, you could trust that source of information.

Firstly, to be abundant, you need to exist—you have that one already!

Secondly, to be abundant, you need to *want* to be so. You need to be really clear, without hesitation or desire to pull it back. Now, this is the area where some of us struggle to find the belief in ourselves and therefore diminish our input to the creation of our truth and abundance. If we don't believe in ourselves, we consequently may not believe in our worth for abundance or, in fact, that abundance is something valid to exist in our space at all.

If you believe everything comes to those who wait, you are in charge of the time you need to wait to receive *everything!* If you think it will be one day, then it will be. If you think it is absolutely conceivable for it to be tomorrow, then that is equally arrangeable for the universe.

That is the law of attraction, for one to conceive of the universal plan of possibilities. If you can conceive it, it just arrives intact and available. Sometimes, it doesn't look exactly as we imagined, so we need to be able to recognize it, but believe that it arrives nonetheless. It will be perfect and in exact proportion to what you envisaged in its return to you. That is the law of our space. You must receive exactly the same as you believe, conceive, and incur.

Be kind to yourself, therefore, and think positively—this is a basic principle of abundance! You are first with Creator in your universe. If you are not kind to yourself, who else can be? You must create your reality in perfect proportion to your understanding of greatness in your and the universe's loving plan. Be light to receive light! Rainbows are for everyone; they are not exclusive to some.

Do you think it is selfish to want for yourself? How can it be if you are building from the ground up? You begin your universe and your connection to Source, and all of that can be considered the greater good.

WHAT IS THE GREATER GOOD?

The greater good is everything both universal and on this planet beyond yourself to which you have some form of influence or which you can perceive. Therefore, if you can conceive of it in thought, you can influence it. Quantum physics talks of the principles of light and watching light. If you watch light, it changes from particles to waves. Your thoughts are just as measurable as a frequency as everything else you can see.

You think; therefore, you are!

If you want to assist the greater good, you can think positively and look for ways to facilitate positive action in your own space. You can donate to charities, smile at someone, and "pay it forward" so to speak. You can treat someone with respect, you can try a new skill, and you can involve yourself in your child's life and interests. You can be someone you are proud of any day you want to. You are in charge; don't forget. Therefore, you are, to some extent, in control of your environment, even if you don't always get everything you want because you are connected to the free will of others with whom you intersect. You are still in charge of the way in which you choose to intersect in any given space.

If creation loves you, you are already valid, and therefore, you are already gifted. You have free will; you can choose to use that will for good or to ignore your own best instincts.

What do we as a society put emphasis on and view with respect or with kudos?

We can influence the way the world views situations and influence the group consciousness by our own thoughts. We can influence what the world emphasises by our own actions and thoughts. You can connect to Creator and ask to facilitate greater good work within your environment, and your thoughts and light can carry that action into being. This is true empowerment within the framework of free will. So it stands to reason that learning to simplify this process and enact it with some form of absolute direction would be helpful if you really wanted to change this world and empower your space.

In my workshop How to Connect to That which Created You, I show you how to use your innate abilities to facilitate and enact an absolutely evident connection to that universal source. You learned to facilitate this greater good work and to enact healings for yourself, others, and this beautiful planet of ours.

In my more advanced workshops, I show you how to broaden your perception to include all levels of your soul and the universe in general. I teach you how to connect to animals, crystals, and other angelic beings that exist around us in all ways. This form of existence, where these things are daily normality, is such a wonderful and facilitating gift. It is empowering to receive information from "the horse's mouth"; to really speak with God, creation, and angels and other beings; to *be* in your own life with a sense of purpose and connection.

Please help our network of humanity to interconnect with each other and Source so our free will can facilitate positive abundance and goodwill for all. This is the message I have heard and would like to deliver, because that is my mission here. It is my passion to teach and deliver the Word directly. The environment is safe, light, and joyful when you have no fear of your own empowerment.

Creator states that "where Empowerment is Present, Fear is not." Wisdom, indeed!

WHAT IS LIGHT?

Light is obviously a form of energy that can be seen. Light energy can be converted to grow plants and help us to see and observe our environment. Creation energy is *the light*.

From our earth-based understanding of light, we know it can present in particles called photons, which are unobservable by the naked eye. We know that light, when observed, forms a wave pattern that can travel through space.

Light waves can present in different colours and densities, depending on the frequency. We can use Creator's light and colour to heal by connecting to Creator and asking to have a colour frequency passed through an object to heal it, for example. The colour and frequency differ according to the individual need in any healing. If you buy a book on colour, you can see that esoterically and from chakra charts, colour relates to different meanings and body zones as well. For example, in a chakra chart, the colour blue relates to the throat chakra. The colour blue has many potential meanings, but it is often related to communication, peace, tranquillity, or protection, depending on the hue or tint of the blue we are describing. Yellow, as per the solar plexus chakra (at the point where the ribs meet), is often related to joy and abundance. As all colour has the directly opposite potential, yellow can also represent anxiety and fear. You can buy comprehensive books that describe colour and its meanings. You will have your own sense of what colour means for you. I have provided a new chakra chart and a section explaining the chakras in the next chapter in order to assist you with the basic body zone references for colour healing purposes. Please note, there is an eighth chakra notated with new information channelled directly from Creator.

Whilst connected to Creator, you can just visualize a colour healing by allowing the pictures to present and Creator to choose the colours required. You only need to observe the light, and the witnessing of this will enact the healing potential of whatever colour or light is given.

The speed of light is a physical constant; it is the speed at which electromagnetic radiation travels in a vacuum. Its value is 299,792,458 metres per second. This constant is significant in the understanding and study of astronomy and space travel, to name two of the fields that use this formula.

We already know that light travels at approximately 299,000 kilometres per second and light from the sun takes about eight minutes to travel to Earth, which is approximately 150 million kilometres away. Our science tells us that within this solar system, distance and time are relevant.

When connected to Creator, the mere process of enacting a thought to request a healing defies these known, internally manifested laws and it manifests instantly in the universal knowledge. The process will obey, to some extent, the internal law factor of taking a bit of time and space to become completed, in our time and reality.

EXPLAINING CHAKRAS

Chakra, in the ancient Sanskrit language, means spinning wheel or vortex. Originally, it was the description of a chariot wheel. Chakras are spinning vortexes that rotate alternately clockwise and anticlockwise down the length of the body. It is the opposite rotation sequence for males than females. Males commence clockwise from the crown, and females commence anti-clockwise.

Ancient healers described the chakras or energy centres in studies and written work. These descriptions have been traced to approximately 2,600 years ago. It is not surprising to note that the studies have now been demonstrated to be anatomically correct.

Information was presented that displayed the location of seven chakras on the physical body, siting them as follows.

The first five chakra points are located at the site of the five main nerve ganglia of the spinal column, where the nerve endings form junctions. At these nerve ganglia, nerves from different organs and parts of the body join to the spinal cord. These chakras are named from base to throat by their common names as:

1. First or Root Chakra,
2. Second, Navel, Hara, or Sacral Chakra
3. Third or Solar Plexus Chakra
4. Fourth or Heart Chakra
5. Fifth or Throat Chakra

The other two chakras are sited at the upper and lower areas of the brain.

6. Sixth or Third Eye Chakra
7. Seventh or Crown Chakra

I have been given channelled information on the Eighth Chakra, which I present for the first time for you in print. How exciting!

8. Eighth or Earth Connection Chakra

This relates specifically to the relationship between the feet and the Earth grounding.

Each chakra is also associated with one of the seven endocrine glands.

This demonstrates that each organ, the entire body, and its functions are connected to our chakras by the nervous system and the endocrine systems of the body.

CHAKRAS VIBRATE

All matter vibrates, from atoms to planets millions of light years away. Electrons move around the nucleus of an atom. Planets revolve around their suns. All frequencies are generated from the movement of matter in this universe. All molecules within each atmosphere are interconnected. The group consciousness of thought within each gravitational environment of every dense planet and mass is interconnected and vibrating. As anything moves, it therefore vibrates. Wherever its location and whatever its purpose, it is generating frequency waves. Where there is vibration, there is sound and colour. Every part of our body vibrates at a specific sound and, therefore, aligned colour frequency.

As I have demonstrated before in this text, as each of the eight chakras has a specific sound associated with it, it must also have a colour vibration and a frequency of thought and emotion. That is why the use of colour and sound can return balance to our chakras, bringing the vortex back to health via the perfect frequency calibration.

WHAT HAPPENS IF A CHAKRA IS OUT OF BALANCE?

As is normal in all magnetic or frequency situations of balance, it is important to keep the chakra vortex in the correct balanced and calibrated functioning order. Sounds complicated, doesn't it? *Calibrated* is a term used to describe a finely tuned mechanism, needing to be set or vibrate at a very specific mathematical formula. Our chakras are naturally attuned to the correct frequency for the specific vibration and meaning of the chakra vortex at the site of the body. When we become "out of tune," we can adjust the calibration and spin of the vortex unintentionally by our distorted emotions, exposure to EMF (electromagnetic frequencies), drugs and medications, and even rock concerts! Many disturbing emotions or interactions may upset our equilibrium.

You can have a major fight with your spouse and find your solar plexus chakra, heart chakra, throat chakra, and base chakra immediately affected. The Hara or Navel Chakra, which is physically sited over the umbilicus, plays a part in digestion and also in the gut emotions. We have heard people say, "I feel gutted," as an example.

Why would a chakra vortex be able to maintain balance if your emotions are all over the place? The resulting feelings of anxiety and stress upset the naturally balanced frequency of the chakra. They vibrate more densely than normal if anger or stress is present. The lower chakras are particularly susceptible to upset if you have a disconnection with a loved one or if you harbor resentments. The circular vortex pattern, once out of sync, can being to spin in an oval pattern, out of alignment, or can rotate in the wrong frequency sporadically.

The throat chakra is blocked if we cannot speak our mind. We may develop disease of the voice-box area, affecting the thyroid, which is located in the same zone as the throat chakra.

Self-esteem and self-worth issues are often linked with throat chakra distortions. If we cannot express or communicate properly, the chakra vortex is out of balance and we develop the potential for disruption in that chakra. Any stagnancy of a vortex energy will invert into the physical tissue and produce a potential disease. Tonsillitis, thyroid problems, glands being swollen, throat infections, speech problems like stuttering, basic communication difficulties, and sore throats or laryngitis may occur. Do you get the picture?

By the term "*dis*-ease" I mean "lack of ease," predisposing the body to distorted energy. When the body's energy is distorted, dis-ease occurs, otherwise known as disease or illness.

Imagine any of the chakras of the body, over the location on the chart, and you can already imagine a potential flood of diseases, which may occur in the specific zone of the physical, following the above principles. It is the basis of most modern disease diagnoses to treat the symptoms of the disorder but ignore the origin of the energetic disruption or the dis-ease input specific to the time prior to the symptoms manifesting. An alternative, or holistic, practitioner is more likely to ask you what happened in the time frame immediately prior to you noticing that you were displaying symptoms of dis-ease. They will work with you to understand the process of induction into the current imbalance.

We can correct dis-ease and stagnation potentials early if we recognize the need to do so and ask for the appropriate balancing to be done by Creator. It is preferable to correct the imbalance in the specific chakra the moment an event occurs and causes an imbalance or as soon as it is recognised.

Remember, when resourcing the following charts, which are provided for your interest, you may be inclined to focus on any areas you feel are out of balance at the moment in order to identify your own function or dysfunction patterns. The key to using the chart with wisdom is to note where and in what pattern an organ or systemic problem you may be encountering is located.

Next, check the specific information provided for the chakra aligned to that physical location on your own body. You may choose to use the tone provided to chant out the dis-ease or attempt to balance the chakra. You can connect to Creator, ask for balance of the chakra, and watch for probable future shifts in the dis-ease pattern of any organ located in that chakra vicinity.

You will be able to access understanding about the core issues involved in disruption of that chakra energy. These are identification tools to help you in your *now* to identify any problem areas and to give you knowledge and understanding to progress into *ease* in the chakra zone.

Good luck and blessings in your playtime with the chakra charts. Have some fun, and remember that you are not a category, but an individual. As such, you don't have to specifically fit each and every paradigm listed. However, as you are a child of God, you are likely to fit the "human paradigm blueprint" somewhere. You may find great benefit from the ability to identify and gain some knowledge and control of any concerns and build belief systems to light in your own chakra systems.

EIGHT CHAKRAS CHART
FOR EASY REFERENCE

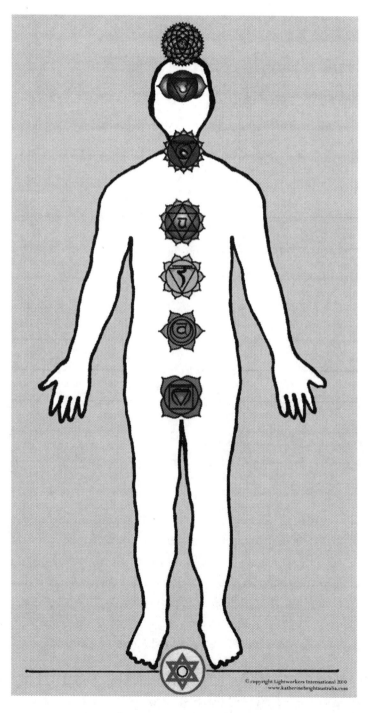

© Katherine and Kim Bright 2009

Common Name: First or Base Chakra

Sanskrit name: *Muladhara* (root)

Location: Base of spine, at the seat of Kundalini

Colour: Red

Essential oils: Patchouli, cedar wood, sandalwood, ylang-ylang

Relevant crystal energies: Garnet, ruby, agate, onyx, hematite, red jasper, black tourmaline, smoky quartz, bloodstone, red coral

Planets and astrological signs: Planets—Mars, Pluto, and Saturn; signs of Aries, Taurus, Scorpio, and Capricorn

Tone: Lam

Core issue: Lack of abundance; repression; denial of self and one's place on the planet; aggression; self-acceptance; alleviation of worries; placement

Element: Earth

Endocrine glands: Sexual and adrenal

Body relationship: Base of spine; colon/rectum; digestive elimination; sustenance of physical body; sexual system; reproductive organs; flowing with Earth-nature—bladder

If overvalued, may lead to: Sexual fetishism; manipulation and withdrawal of unconditional love and support to others; excessive masturbation; need to punish those with whom you have altercations or disagreements; revenge.

If undervalued, may lead to: Fatigue; loss of self-comprehension and feeling lost; dislocation from the Earth; difficulty placing oneself; no sense of direction physically and emotionally; spiritually bereft of rite of passage to move forward with approval of the Earth; searching excessively for approval from others; lack of appetite; diminished responsibility for finances; fear; sexual dysfunction (for example, lack of desire); feelings of cold in the extremities and poor ability of the body to control temperature; neediness, poverty mentality; complaining or being whiney; overcompensating in social gatherings because of inadequacy feelings.

Spiritual challenges: How well we manage our physical world, the ability to remain "grounded" and trust that our abundance is provided by the Earth

Second, Navel, Hara, or Sacral Chakra

Sanskrit name: *Svadhisthana* (sweetness)

Location: Lower abdomen

Colour: Orange

Essential oils: Bergamot, geranium, rosemary, sandalwood, jasmine, rose

Relevant crystal energies: Amber, citrine, topaz, moonstone, fire agate, orange spinel, gaspite, fire opal

Planets and astrological signs: Moon, the planets Venus and Pluto, and the signs of Libra, Cancer, and Scorpio

Tone: Vam

Core issues: Repression of one's true nature; nurturing issues and eating disorders; knowing how to be oneself in the company of others; being fed by our own truth; survival, neediness, or the need of support; knowing without a doubt that we belong; understanding creation in our world is acceptable to our walking forward; assimilation of incoming information and the ability to discern truth; feeling safe; lack of fear

Element: Water

Endocrine gland: Pancreas

Body relationship: Ovaries, reproductive organs, uterus; basis of self-esteem and therefore stress patterns; entire digestive system prior to rectum; intestines; digestive secretions; blood; abdominal musculature; lower spine and pelvis; the kidneys, appendix, pancreas, and liver

If overvalued, may lead to: Overeating; distortion of body image; overcompensating for unsuccessful relationships by overindulgent behaviours; playing the field in sexual relationships at one's own expense for validation; digestive dyspepsia; burning gut syndromes where inflammation plays a part; logistical nightmares and dramas perpetuating one's space; inability to settle anywhere in a location, job, relationship, or viewpoint; hot-body syndrome including hot flushes with menopause being more pronounced; difficulty interpreting people's thoughts, responses, and agendas; irritability of the bowel and digestive organs due to excessive stimulation of energies;

extreme sadness, guilt, or feelings of sorrow due to suffering from prior events in one's life; anger, rage or conditions where we cannot accept balance is our normal state

If undervalued, may lead to: Lack of sustenance and biological difficulty absorbing nutrients; perpetual sorrow; feeling deprived of basic human rights; lack of perseverance and mentality to give up "because it won't work anyway"; feelings of being driven mad by one's digestive system; overload emotionally; relationship difficulties due to feeling impassive; lack of interest in participation; confusion about identity of self in one's own life and home environment; basic deprivation of energy (done by the self to the self); could involve food behaviours like eating disorders; feeling overwhelmed by finances or life demands; "can't see the wood for the trees"; slow metabolism; lack of joyful expression and participation in creative pursuits; feelings of religious persecution.

Spiritual challenges: Control and dominance issues; overindulging the fear of relationship and confronting solidarity of self where one feels weakened by aloneness; the ability to *be* constructively and in this world supported by and nurtured by that which spirit provides

Third or Solar Plexus Chakra

Sanskrit name: *Manipura* (lustrous gem)

Location: Solar plexus, below the diaphragm

Colour: Yellow

Essential oils: Clary-sage, thyme, pine, juniper, lavender, rosemary

Relevant crystal energies: Citrine, amber, tiger's eye, peridot, yellow tourmaline, yellow topaz, yellow calcite

Planets and astrological signs: Sun; the planets Mercury, Jupiter, and Mars; and the signs of Leo, Sagittarius, and Virgo

Tone: Ram

Core issues: Fear; guilt; anonymity; fear of exposing oneself; understanding of how we fit in the world; being with others; threats; interpreting our environment as friendly or otherwise; happiness with the soul; self-awareness; anxiety or comfort-zone issues; nervous system relationship . . . jumpiness

Element: Fire

Endocrine glands: The pancreas and the adrenal

Body relationship: The large intestine; spleen; liver; stomach; gastrointestinal upsets; abdominal core musculature; diaphragm; ribs; ability to breathe; midback; pancreas; adrenal glands; the nervous system; hormonal regulation; gall production (gallbladder)

If overvalued, may lead to: Overconfident attitude; opulence in one's personal environment being mandatory; no sense of proportion; vague about obligations to self and others; inability to comply because of dysfunction; unable to assess accurately what is required to cope in any given situation; extreme stress; anxiety or nervous irritability; insomnia; abusive behaviour; manipulation to gain one's need for safety; obvious boasting; basic and unusual behaviour (in respect of social etiquette due to overcompensation of ego); dark thoughts and suicidal tendency; obsessive-compulsive disorders and neuroses; demanding nature

If undervalued, may lead to: Thwarted ambition; perverse need to hide from responsibility and a withdrawn mental state; depressive conditions that involve heavy use of medications as the norm; basic insecurity about most things; self-denial; secluding oneself out of fear of reprisals; hermit-like behaviour for any safety-related reason; stomach disorders leading to eating behaviours that are irregular; irritability; moroseness; dominance or aggression towards anyone trying to shift you from your firmly held beliefs; disquiet; closeting oneself away including excessive need to stay in bed and be alone; vitamin and mineral deficiencies due to lack of absorption in the intestinal tract; lack of nurturing experiences; inability to fall pregnant; endocrine disturbances; panic attacks

Spiritual challenges: Maturing of the ego; living in empowerment; dismissing anxiety as superfluous; trust issues of self and others with whom we have initially forged our personal ego, particularly relationships with the major players in our personal journey and especially parental control issues, including our personal acceptances; trusting the path of spirituality and trusting ourselves to fulfil our destiny without harm or neglect

Fourth or the Heart Chakra

Sanskrit name: *Anahatra* (unstruck)

Location: Chest, heart, cardiac plexus

Colour: Green and pink

Essential oils: Lotus, geranium, sandalwood, rose, cedar wood

Remedy recipes: Water made from distilled wattle blossoms, small amount of charcoal for soaking up toxins

Relevant crystal energies: Rose quartz, emerald, jade, aventurine, malachite, rhodolite, dioptase

Planets and astrological signs: The planets Venus and Saturn, the Sun, and the signs Libra, Leo, and Sagittarius

Tone: Yam

Core issues: Being oneself; loving and being loved; being a part of a great passion; loving or being comfortable with one's relationships; wanting to a be a part of a greater good; love in all ways; rejection fears; being able to communicate and be heard by others with acceptance and appreciation; belonging; family ethics; comprehension of our true reasons for being will allow balance and warmth leading to a healthy heart space

Element: Air

Endocrine glands: The thymus gland

Body relationship: Heart disorders and disease (endocrine system linkage); circulatory system, lungs, bronchial tubes, lymphatic system; solar plexus imbalance (heart issues often being linked to anxiety disorders); shoulders and arms; diaphragm; thymus gland; the immune system; the skin; the upper back

If overvalued, may lead to: Possessiveness; fixations in another's space; irregular heart rhythms; hyperactivity; basic motivations being overly focused on emotions; difficult attitude to spouse; self-absorption; overindulgence in wardrobe or imagery, which one feels supports one's identity without needing to be that way; sadness; inability to cope; perception difficulties; striving to be what we are not; lack of self-esteem; feelings of being affronted; breathing difficulties, including asthma attacks; alienation; deprived emotional communication, as you cannot participate without adrenal responses making the heart react, such as a thumping beat, high blood pressure, or rage

If undervalued, may lead to: Lack of compassion; denial of one's needs on all levels; heart disturbances, including arrhythmia; relationship sadness and emotional stress and strain; difficulty communicating one's perceptions and needs; feelings of aloneness leading to loneliness and isolation; decrying that anything is good in life; spiritual dissatisfaction; jealousy and harmful feelings like bitterness; sorrow leading to the need to be alone; separation; disempowerment; fatigue

Spiritual challenges: To learn compassion; the value of forgiveness and unconditional love; that the ego will give way to the heart's true understanding of ethical maturity and growth.

Fifth or Throat Chakra

Sanskrit name: *Vissudha* (purification)

Location: Throat

Colour: Blue

Essential oils: Lavender, basil, cedar wood, juniper

Relevant crystal energies: Blue, topaz, lapis lazuli, aquamarine, sodalite, turquoise, sapphire, blue lace agate, blue tourmaline, blue quartz

Planets and astrological signs: Planets Venus, Mercury, Uranus, and Mars and the signs of Taurus, Gemini, and Aquarius

Tone: Ham

Core issues: Speaking with conviction and acceptance; knowing how to communicate even if untaught by society; being an acceptable part of a group; valued as a speaker; wanting to participate in greater action as a team member; self-reflective value; appreciation of one's inner voice; being heard; being understood; delivery of accurate frequency modulation so toning and words are really accepted; wanting to understand therefore being deliberately accurate in our delivery to others for a higher purpose; flow

Element: Ether—Akasa

Endocrine glands: The thyroid and parathyroid gland

Body relationship: Speech; throat; thyroid and parathyroid glands; airways; swallowing; chewing of food, therefore affecting digestion; ears and Eustachian tubes; sinus to mouth; salivary glands; tonsils; musculature of the neck; thoracic and cervical spine; shoulder blades; shoulder girdle; collarbone; base of skull—occipital region; teeth, gums, and jaw; temporomandibular joint; nose; lymphatics; tongue

If overvalued, may lead to: Overtalking; lack of content in one's speech but overly interested in hearing oneself speak (getting carried away with our cosmic rabbiting); inflammation of the throat, including tonsillitis; tongue swellings; glandular disturbances; oral thrush or ulcerations; gossiping; jaw misalignments through stubborn clenching; opinionatedness; difficulty knowing when to choose to speak and when silence would be preferential; self-centeredness; acidity of the mouth, tongue, and throat areas

If undervalued, may lead to: Inability to express one's truth with the words and voice; fear of singing; fear of being heard; weakness of attitude when speaking or offering an opinion; self-esteem being low and fearing that you will be rejected in your opinions so refusing to speak and express at all or doing so rarely; diminished function of the glands in the throat and therefore low thyroid activity; rotting of the teeth; nerve pain or neuralgia of teeth, neck, and jaw areas, including ears and specifically ear infections and pain; fear of reprisals; neck pain; repetitive strain injury in the arms coming from the shoulder girdle as the body holds stress here; pain in general related to self-esteem and withdrawn energies

Spiritual challenges: The ability for right action, truth, and validity of correct communication and speech; to understand how to communicate ethically and in God's light; being and trusting that the universe will flow through your speech centre and provide the nurturing thought and frequency that others need to hear from you; confidence issues about trusting your gut reactions to truth and balance in spirit and life; communicating your trust in spiritual Zen and integrity to others. You *are*; therefore, you *be*!

Sixth or the Third Eye Chakra

Sanskrit name: *Ajna* (to perceive)

Location: The centre of the forehead, brow

Colour: Indigo

Essential oils: Lavender, rosemary, peppermint, spearmint

Relevant crystal energies: Sodalite, amethyst, lapis lazuli, azurite, fluorite, lapidolite

Planets and astrological signs: The planets Jupiter, Uranus, Mercury, and Neptune and signs Sagittarius, Aquarius, and Pisces

Tone: Ham-ksham

Core issues: Acceptability as a seer; acknowledging one's inner voice and perception; the knowing; holding firm in one's convictions of spiritual grace and purpose; lack of fear about delivery of greater good messages; knowledge from the etheric willingly followed and graced; interpretation

Element: Light

Endocrine glands: The pituitary and the pineal gland

Body relationship: Migraine; cranial tension; sore eyebrow bones; forehead bulging; mind/spirit cognisance; brain; forebrain uptake of knowledge (frontal lobe); experience through the skin (sense of touch); eyes; sinuses; face; the pineal and pituitary gland

If overvalued, may lead to: Overwhelm on a psychic level; inability to differentiate between reality and the spirit world in another dimension as they intermingle sporadically, maintaining a confused space; possible delusions of grandeur as a psychic leading to diminished accuracy of information received; disconnectedness from the Earth plane; worry and anxiety about being persecuted as a psychic being; denial of our third-dimensional plane's validity as a reality; overuse of skills leading to spiritual burnout and compulsions; no value for peace and quiet and the silence of Zen; overperformance and production of spiritual media with the possibility of undervaluing the creative content thereby producing inaccurate perceptive work

If undervalued, may lead to: Difficulties with the eyes because we don't wish to "see"; psychic withdrawal and denial of skill base and perceptions; being underwhelmed by our spiritual connection leading to scepticism; denial of God's existence; perpetual sadness about our disconnection from our Creator; inability to perceive with any instinctiveness or intuition; separation from our higher knowing; fear of reprisals; basically wearing thin and being tired mentally; desire to escape from the spiritual insights we receive; choosing death rather than visions persisting; schizophrenia

Spiritual challenges: Pride and the ability to make judgments; second sight and not falling into past-life challenges of visibility and trust; if you have been a seer in any lifetime, the third eye has been very active—trusting in the compatibility of your third eye "knowledge" in this modern age may be an issue; acknowledgement that the visions of spirit provided to you are not your imagination

Seventh or Crown Chakra

Sanskrit name: *Sahasrara* (thousandfold)

Location: The crown of the skull

Colour: White, magenta

Essential oils: Chamomile, orange, lime, cinnamon, nutmeg mixed with lavender, frankincense

Relevant crystal energies: Diamond, clear quartz, selenite, pyrite, fluorite, kyanite, gypsum, white amethyst

Planets and astrological signs: The planets Saturn and Neptune, the signs Capricorn and Pisces

Tone: Om

Core issues: Connection to the Greater Source; being able to communicate with the higher aspects of self and etheric beingness; wanting to be connected to the spiritual realm, which provides complete sustenance to our spirit; wisdom from above to the self; being able to harness universal knowledge; connection to God

Element: Thought

Endocrine glands: The tonsils . . . why? . . . a direct nervous link from the pineal gland to the speech centre confuses the chakra matrix into believing that the ability to speak and converse directly with creation is necessary and therefore links the nervous system directly to the glands of the throat or the fifth chakra system influences

Body relationship: Skull; hair; mind (state of mind and thought processes); pineal gland; parasympathetic nervous system; cerebral cortex of the brain; skeleton; heart and lungs (how one's connection to spirit affects the heart/lung meridian on a spiritual level, predisposing the body to a response in the organs concerned)

If overvalued, may lead to: Feelings of being overwhelmed by light; headaches and inability to stand light—seeing it as an interference; migraines; feeling bombarded by thoughts and insights; skeletal pain, osteoporosis, and bone disorders due to excessively misaligned input from our mind separating our body from our spirit; obsessive religious philosophies as we perceive our way to be the only way and all others as wrong; denial of grace and peace, preferring instead to dwell on superiority

If undervalued, may lead to: Degradation of philosophy of kindness to all mankind; persecution priority; dominance and leading the way to defile another; delusions of grandeur but lack of insight in actuality; slow thought processes; lack of comprehension of the "greater good" in any issue; being pernickety; slow reflexes; learning difficulties; rigid belief systems; domination of others; ego-based guruism; feelings of spiritual superiority through lack of insight into *the One*

Spiritual challenges: Belief in God and connection to the entirety of the universal plan in your secret inner consciousness; knowing that your higher self is in full operation ethically with your genetic body and you are safe within your physical body spiritually to explore highest consciousness; *trusting* the presence of the angels and spiritual realm to provide for your abundance

Eighth Chakra . . . Earth Connection Chakra

Sanskrit Name: *Alanjieaea*—pronounced "alanyia"(to carry forth a resonance)

Location: Between the soles of the feet and the ground

Colour: Jasper brown

Essential oils: Frankincense

Relevant crystal energies: Red jasper, agate, tourmaline, hematite, pyrite, white quartz, rainbow tourmaline, Australian zebra stone

Planets and astrological signs: Earth, relevant to all signs of the zodiac

Tone: Om

Core issues: Grounding, alleviation of lack of abundance; respect for Mother Earth; clarity of vision of the soul's true purpose upon the Earth plane

Element: Earth

Endocrine glands: Spleen

Body relationship: Feet and legs; walking on the earth (bushwalking is very nurturing); abundance and therefore weight issues; nurturing by Earth so skeletal system in its entirety; spleen and lymphatics relating to ability of the body to shed toxins

If overvalued, may lead to: Self-indulgent behaviour; bizarre need to acquire monetary wealth; lack of concern for the planet and those who inhabit it; lack of care of animals and pets; egoisms and use of self-indulgent language designed to support falsely built inflated ideas of one's own space; need to acquire . . . anything!

If undervalued, may lead to: Bone abnormalities and lack of abundance; no idea who we are and loss of truth in personal identity; fear and worry for the planet, which becomes obsessive or a misguided compulsion to save oneself from harm; lack of energy; sleepy nature; loss of tenacity and belief in a better world; fear of loss of physical possessions, home, and hearth; fear of separation from grounded family or if from an abusive home environment, then fear of repeated abuse; fear of bureaucratic interference in one's wishes for truth in one's own home

Spiritual challenges: To maintain a mindfulness to Zen and graceful behaviour; allowing flow and going with the flow instead of striving to make things happen in our own time frame; indulging that which is against the belief that spirit will provide if we only ask for it and then allowing the letting go of our manifestations so the greater good can prevail; to allow our secret selves to become a focus where we try to hide from others our truth and the beliefs we find supportive; we must have faith, not only in God, but also in ourselves and our ability to provide for ourselves without struggle; *trust*, also trust Earth provides

WHAT HAPPENS WHEN YOU TALK TO GOD?

Who or what is God, creation, Source, the one?

It is the age-old question that we want answered. We feel both connected and distanced in our communication from that omnipotent presence sometimes.

We have been told who God is by our religious faiths. Depending on the faith concerned, the image may differ.

For me, the connection is very personal. My creation experience is mine alone, so I can only tell you from my perception. Yours will be uniquely yours. If you are shown, in a simple manner, how to connect to that magnificent energy, you can form your own conclusions, interactions, and visions with the energy that is so overwhelmingly in favour of light and beingness, joy and laughter.

When I connect, I sometimes see visions, imagery, light, and colour and hear music. Sometimes I see angels, beings, and feel a sense of the solar system. Often, I get a blank screen but hear a voice. The voice is not my own, although, as my mind's imagination is used to interpret the frequency of the information being sent to me, I assume it has some feeling of being like my own voice. It is as I perceive my own sound to be.

Creation speaks to me in sentences. They are very specifically worded sentences that carry a nuance of frequency in the words, which makes the intention very exact. There is absolutely no mistaking the words used and the intention created. I am very definitely aware it isn't me talking to myself, however, as the information is of a different nature to my normal thinking patterns. It may contain words I don't normally use, and often, the information is beyond my own conceptualization in its content.

INTENTION

Intention is a very important thing in our lives. I don't believe we comprehend the full nuances in our general society of how we create with this intention in all things to which we allude. Because of free will, we are given the empowerment to create for ourselves whatever it is we believe is right for us or which we believe we deserve, or don't deserve. Often the best manifestations come when you are just convinced of your space or thoughts. You don't have to ritualise or invent a process to intend. Just allow your thoughts to provide in "the now" for you and your space. Don't boundary what you can conceive by trying to organise the outcome or by trying to force the space of thought into action. Knowing creates reality. Suspicion detracts from the ability to believe and to therefore draw towards yourself great things because you have already told the universe your intention is to disbelieve or be unable to conceive of change for yourself. Perhaps you think it is impossible and therefore it becomes your manifest to go without. Creator is not boundaried by this reality on Earth. The universe has infinite capacity.

If infinity exists, nothing is impossible and abundance is the thought pattern of Creation. If you intend, the universe is compelled to listen. If you intend for light and goodness, the universe is respectful of your free will and can enact for you. You become intentionally interactive. You only have to ask with good intention for connection to creation, and you can facilitate a positive shift immediately. We exist in gravity on this planet and are bound by the sixth dimension's laws of gravity, time, and space. What this means, in effect, is that our intention is manifest instantly in creation. Manifestations of intent may take a little time to physically present themselves, considering circumstances of our free will, time and space, and our interactions with others on this planet. However, once intended in a let-go-and-let-God way, asking in Creator's profound wisdom for assistance, all considerations and actions manifest for the greater good in their own time and way, without you needing to fear that something will be lost or distorted along the way. This is very empowering to consider—to know that our thought projections can become reality instantly and then to allow ourselves to just flow with the aspects of consideration in our connectedness to time and space here on Earth.

If you intend whilst connected to creation in the way I demonstrate in this book and in my workshops, you float your thoughts out of Earth's gravitational pull and your mind will enter the theta-brainwave state. This brainwave takes our consciousness out of our physical reality and into the creation plane. You can then alter space and time in your intention, and project for change in your physical *now*.

Intrigued yet? I would love to introduce you to this theory, here in print, and let you taste it. Then, if you wish to play with this, you may consider some assistance via workshopping with the meditations, et cetera.

The Process:

Imagination is often our biggest ally in intending connection, and often, we deny our messages from spirit because we think we could be imagining them!

How else can we be spoken to by spirit, so that the mind conceives it or our senses interpret it? Don't be scared of your imagination or failure. Allowing imagery or sensory experience is a key here. By not blocking, you see, as you already have all the skills inbuilt into your beingness. We are not trying to learn anything new; we are just unblocking our perception that it is new!

HOW TO CONNECT TO CREATOR
FOR HEALING AND ASSISTANCE

The first part of connecting to Creator is to **trust** *the process* and *your* **worthiness** *to be connected to Creator.* If you doubt this, or think it is hard, you may make what is an easy process seem difficult. *It is easy to connect to Creator. The ability is inbuilt to all beings!* You are not trying to do anything new. You are really just unblocking what has remained a silent gift. Firstly, you use your imagination to gift yourself with vision.

This is no different to visualizing something you remember; for example, you can remember what your house looks like. By taking your imagination along for a ride with your thoughts, you automatically project your intentions and *just do it.*

Knowing what you sense is visualizing. Visualising is not only seeing any pictures you may see. Visualising is using all your senses of sight, taste, smell and knowing and allowing your intuitive senses to interpret. Your consciousness goes along for the ride to where you point your thoughts and intent.

Visualize or imagine yourself focusing your attention in a place in the earth below your feet. Next, take your consciousness upward into the soles of your feet, up your body, and up to a point on the top of your head. Next, focus on this place and visualize a ball of light sitting on the top of your head (any shape, colour, or size). Imagine yourself inside this light. Next, you say, or think, with this intention:

"Creator, I pray with my full intent to be connected to you now."

Now, allow yourself to relax. Imagine travelling with your thoughts to a bright and relaxing light state, which is when you will be connected. Just knowing you are there will place you there, even if you are unsure. Remember, your intent carries everything.

How we perceive that place of spirit will be an individual thing. We may feel ourselves in a lighter mind-frame state . . . a bit "spacey" perhaps. We may see a brightening of our light if we look up with our eyes closed.

We may not, but if we find our mind too involved, the usual human tendency is to try too hard. My advice is just to know the process and trust that your knowing will place you in connection, because that is all that is really required. And if we think ourselves up and out, above the sky, we automatically focus our attention to a place that is outside Earth's gravitational pull. This allows us to enter the theta-brainwave state easily. It is just a knowing, which is all you need to trust it is working. Don't doubt, as this is "the ego's last stand" in blocking what is actually easy to achieve.

WHAT TO DO ONCE YOU HAVE CONNECTED

When you have connected, you ask for what it is you intend—for example . . .

"Creator, I pray with my full intent that you heal me now, in your profound wisdom of what is needed. Thank you. I know it is done."

Or:

"Creator, I pray with intent that you clear 'this anxiety' from me now, wherever it exists and is appropriate to be cleared, and I then pray for all knowledge and light to be given to me now, which will rebalance me. Thank you. It is done."

You can see by this prayer or intention example above that any intention has parts to it.

Firstly, you need to address someone. The words you use can be your own here. You might choose God, Creator, Source, or Infinite Being. It really doesn't matter as long as you can conceive that the universal light and creation as such is addressed.

The next is your statement of intention. This may vary. Once you are practiced, you will see that it feels comfortable to ask for yourself. You have to intend to the creative force, or God, with absolute focus because otherwise you do not give credence to your request.

For example, if you are going to add "Please, God, but I know I am unworthy to receive this," you do lose a little potential and credibility, don't you think? If you think you can do greater good for yourself or another in a request, give it some gusto and ask!

You must never violate anyone's permission in any process of healing or sending of light. It is up to each and every one of us to receive, or not, any light or energy given. Just because you may want to send it to someone doesn't mean it is appropriate.

Please, always add to any prayer, that the intention is understood to be enacted in Creator's profound wisdom of what is appropriate to be sent and received. I always add that the balancing of any energies involved be done, also wherever needed in Creator's profound wisdom. This is because if you truly intend for some healing or light to be sent to any issue, other person, or yourself, perhaps there may be contingencies and circumstances of which you are unaware. These may also need balancing to that healing. Creator will understand this, and if it is your intention, it will be done automatically, even if you have no idea where and what.

Trust, let go, and let God.

You must have an intention action . . . that is, an instruction or an issue to be dealt with.

What to choose? I have listed an example here; however, you may be very specific if you choose.

For example . . . if you have a sore eye, you may intend a healing to it directly using the the wording of the examples as a guide.

If you have a specific issue, you may insert "your anxiety" as perhaps, "my fear of being alone" or "my feelings of inadequacy." It is up to you to ask Creator for help; the only thing that limits you is your own sense of recognition. If you think anything does not serve your highest good anymore, it can be sent up for a healing or clearing in this manner.

Balancings are very important, as you may intersect with another person's energy, by default, if you are dealing with some issues—for example, if you have an anxiety connected to another. As that person's free will is also involved, you must not violate that, and it may be impossible in the moment to ask for his or her verbal permission. Perhaps it may also be inappropriate to the relationship with that person to broach the subject.

The important factor here is that you are dealing with your own life. You are only asking for the highest good for yourself and all energies connected with you. Creator will understand how to balance the other aspects without violation if you keep your head out of the space and hand it over. In creation, sufficient consideration is given to the fact that you understand and have asked for balancing to be done, wherever Creator in profound wisdom understands is appropriate. That gets you out of any difficulties, and your best healing potential will be facilitated.

An additional thing to think about is that when you do any healing or energy shifts on yourself or others, you should ask Creator in his profound wisdom to balance all family members to the shift you have just made. When you do this, there won't be repercussions and they won't give you a hard time.

An extra consideration to remember in general is that balancing your land and house is important also. If this is not done, you sometimes just don't fit to where you live anymore. Ask Creator to do whatever is necessary and appropriate because sometimes you can make quite a big shift in the energy, which needs to be balanced to comfortably interact with the grid lines. Ask Creator to balance you to your land and vice versa, so that you are compatible. This makes the devic realm, the realm of Earth sprites, fairies, and keepers of the land, comfortable also. Be happy in your own space!

To conclude the process, once all energy has resolved and you feel peace and completion, imagine yourself back with Creator. Visualise a pale-blue light vortex coming from Creator to you. Bring the light closely around you in your imagination, and let it spin in a clockwise direction. Once established, imagine this vortex extending down your body, following you to the ground as you bring yourself back into your body, here grounded on Earth. Let the blue-light vortex flow around you until you are aware you have grounded yourself back here. This consolidates your energy back to balance, cleaning out any dross and connections to others with whom you may have interacted in the healing process. Your auric fields will be clean and bright, as the blue-light vortex acts as a filter. It separates you from others, including any negativity, and cleanses your space. You are wholly yourself again, without external baggage. The process is complete.

In my workshop How to Connect to That which Created You, an experiential workshop, I took participants through this process individually so it would not be difficult or mistaken. Now my mentoring is designed specifically to assist you to grow and be empowered to use this technique proficiently and in such a way as you will not fear your own empowerment to do so.

Please look at my website, www.katherinebrightaustralia.com, for more information.

I travel this beautiful planet of ours, to different locations, as part of my work and synchronization is possible.

In the last few years, I have travelled to Peru and Europe for my work, and I am sure my exciting life experiences will take me to other adventures. If it is meant to be, it will be.

Illustration and design © Katherine Bright 2008
Artist: Ria Walters

FREQUENCY

Frequency—a Wave Pattern

When speaking with Creator, I was told that:

"*Frequency* in song is intrinsic to the makeup, vibration, and webbing of all molecular structure. We hold all emotion in the water molecules of our body. We do not need to be destructive upon this earth, for love is the vibration of which all things resonate.

"As soon as we realise this, there will no longer be war or any competition. Competition is superfluous to the energy of unconditional love. Our creative force vibrates only at the essence of unconditional love, in order to bring in all the appropriate frequencies of light and colour."

Frequency—*light and colour* is all that exists, as in a rainbow hue. It holds within it, and in our cells, all the reflective particles that enable the rainbow spectrum of all colours to be reflected within the being.

When we enlighten the being with unconditional love, we enlighten the being fully to the resonance of Creator.

Have you ever considered the way you speak and think?

If all our thoughts vibrate at a frequency equivalent to the density of that thought, then we are a living, breathing frequency capable of influencing our environment, just by the fact that we exist within it.

When you say or project your thoughts into a reality, you influence anyone in the emitted frequency's path. Those who hear or feel your meaning are influenced by the frequency of your words, the tone and colour of your language. They take on the resonance in the intracellular memory of the water molecules in their cells. They receive the vibration and sense the word. This is why language is so descriptive. It needs to carry the meaning and frequency of the intention carried therein.

As an example, if you are angry, you change the tone, speed, and intensity of the frequency of your spoken word, your body language, and your intention. It is unmistakeable to those in your vicinity. You are readable, audible, and a force to be reckoned with. Yes, a force! Frequency also holds the force of your words and thoughts. This is how you emote.

Bearing the above in mind, also consider how you can influence those who hear you by your general demeanour, by the music you play and listen to, and by the amount of static in your environment, for example, the interference caused by barely audible frequencies of electrical/electronic equipment, electromagnetic frequency (EMF) emissions from appliances and mobile phones, or the electrical power box attached to your home. Many, many possibilities exist within our everyday lives for us to experience, first-hand, the essence of frequency and tone and their influence on our emotions and thoughts. Personally, I am very susceptible to EMF emissions in my general environment. I hear the buzz of the power outlets. I am at absolute peace when camping and away from the general hubbub of city life. I can find myself becoming irritable, as if bombarded by some field I can't control though I can definitely feel it and know I am being affected by it.

I use devices on all my appliances to cancel out the EMF problem, in order that my environment remains as peaceful as possible. The brand I use is Gia Wellness, but there are other brands you may find on the Internet to assist you to clean up frequency overload in your personal environment. Check out www.mygiawellness.com/katherinebright.

One of the biggest problems for Western society today is desensitisation of recognition. We are often disrupted by unseen energetic frequencies. Our children are bombarded and so often they switch off to that which upsets their equilibrium. They often don't recognise the potentially unhealthy influence upon them. The TV is often on, as background company, when a parent is busy. Therefore, the child does not receive as much influence and participation in nature as previous generations. Computers and the Internet dictate many waking hours of "enjoyment." Life takes on a sense of unreality. The predominant influence is virtual reality.

Conscience and nature consciousness are in danger of being lost to this generation, unless we remember to be kind to our children and spend time with them. Is it wise for us to be too busy or defer with the "wait a minute" comments that we find necessary to use sometimes in our busy schedules. Food for thought! A child who is spoken with and indulged by informed parents is a child who has the ability to respond to his or her environment in a healthy and empowered way. Create a colourful world of art and interaction with frequencies of health and light. That should be the aim of anyone really wanting to provide health and light to the enlightened world of positivity we could provide on Earth.

As my personal contribution to our local community I have recently become a Scout Leader with Scouts Australia. I have done this to support my young son. He learns healthy, self-esteem boosting skills and we both bond with opportunities to ground ourselves in the environmental pursuits of earth and sea. Time spent nurturing supports us all, especially young people who are forming their knowledge, integrity and self-belief.

ENTRAINMENT

What is entrainment? Put simply, when a wave pattern or frequency exists in any environment, the emotion, thought, or atmosphere is vibrating at a particular density. Anything in the vicinity is drawn to adjust its frequency of thought or emotion to the same wave pattern frequency if it is a strong vibration. The strongest vibration in the area will predominate, and any weaker signals will be drawn to entrain to the same frequency vibration. Therefore, if you are moody, sullen, angry, or irritable and yours is the strongest emotion amongst those in the room with you, the others will be influenced by it and find their frequency adjusting or aligning to it. They may potentially take on the same stance and react with the same density as you. There is the real possibility of influencing others to become irritable or moody as well. However, if another in the room carries a stronger frequency and is more stable, that person's frequency can coerce you to entrain to them. Take, as an example, being jogged out of your irritable demeanour by a family member who persists in "joking you out of it." He or she facilitates in his or her own space, in a happy frame of mind, until you change your frequency and cheer up via the experience of that atmosphere.

Doesn't this make sense? You experience it every day. You may recall being sad when sad music plays or wanting to dance to mambo music. Perhaps, you have even been reminded of times past when a particular song on the radio takes you back energetically to the frequency of the experience of which it reminds you. Yes, frequency is a strong experiential. To recap, the intensity and strength of any frequency will dictate the general frequency of the immediate environment. So, be positive, wherever you are able, in order to generate a positive response in your own environment. You really do create your own reality. Now you may understand better exactly how that works.

TONING YOUR BODY TO YOUR SPECIFIC TONE

Each person's body has a specific healing tone. It is the actual note to which you are attuned. At that note, you vibrate with the most integrity for you. It may be an F sharp, a B, or whatever note. When you are tuned at that specific frequency, your cells are happy. There seems to be joy in the body, and it feels like a balance and alignment within the body.

In order to achieve this, please connect to Creator as per the process you have been shown. Pray to be attuned (like a tuning fork) to the tone to which you are supposed to vibrate for your perfect balance and health.

The intent to use here is:

"Creator, I pray with my full intent that you tone my body to its particular healing tone and rebalance me, my family, my house, and my land to the shift. Thank you."

Watch this enact energetically, as per the process you have been shown in the connection chapter.

Colour, Toning, and Vibrational Healing Essence

As Creator said, "Frequency in song is intrinsic to the makeup, vibration, and webbing of all molecular structure." As humans, we are approximately 70 per cent water and are perfect models of healing via the water molecules of our bodies. We know now that tones, colours, and all vibrational frequencies resonate and create a wave pattern and crystal formations based upon thoughts, emotions, and resonances within the water molecules of our physical bodies. Therefore, as an intention in healing, you can influence the healing within the physical body by passing through it the tone, colour, and thought (e.g., love) desired to achieve a specific result in clearing and balancing. This heals as it balances and clarifies all blocked energy, dispersing it and taking our body forward and closer to the place of divinity. Our body is our temple. How many times do we hear this but ignore it because we do not understand the process by which this truth works?

Remember, Source always knows how to entrain all things to balance. Even homeostasis in the human body demonstrates the example. Your intention is to clear a problem and heal it, with light and Creator's profound wisdom in balance. You must understand that the process of handing over to Creator in trust is necessary. The fact is that all things in this universe are finely balanced, in creation's wisdom.

THE BEST HEALING PROCESS

Holding the intent in all healings, teachings, and balancings that they be done by Creator's wisdom is best. This makes sure clearings and healings are successful in all places, aspects, times, and dimensions simultaneously.

I liked being told by Source that "We do not need to have a separation from the Creator, for we exist simultaneously as the one." To me, this is comforting and truth.

COLOUR, ESSENCE

Another Healing Process with Colour and Frequency

You can request any of the colours of the rainbow to be sent into someone in order to heal and balance him or her. Creator will know which colours or tones are the best for the person's needs each time.

Just hand it over to Creator.

After sending in a colour vibration to clear something, you send in a colour learning in order to balance it.

The knowledge that needs to be there is what Creator will replace it with.

It is called the *colour learning* because the appropriate thoughts, vibrations, or colour will hold the *essence* of what it is that needs to be replaced into the space to clarify it. Remember the *essence* is as Creator understands it. You do not need to become worried or stressed about what the knowledge is. It just is, and the Source always knows what is needed. You do not need specific itemised information for healings to work.

Essence

Essence is an important word to understand. In this case, it means the absolute minutest and most completely perfect frequency, with all meanings and the merest whiff of molecular energy included. All-encompassing in its minutest form.

Essence can be any minute particle or resonance of anything that's been residing in the body or fields and doesn't belong to you. It has to be removed and is not just like cellular memory. You take your intent to include this cellular memory but also the essence that is to be taken because it is very subtle. I imagine it is like minute molecules of matter that can't be described but also don't belong there. So, when you put information in to our beingness at all the levels, the Creator's light encodes with the appropriate essence to fill the gaps.

You simply request that:

"Creator, I pray with intent that you send into me the appropriate colour vibration to heal this problem and follow it with the colour learning to balance it. Thank you. I am aware this is done."

Have some fun experimenting with colour being sent into the body to attune it in this way.

SEVEN STATES OF BEING

"There are seven states of being," Creator says.

The seven states of being are:

1. Love,
2. Harmony,
3. Matter,
4. Energy,
5. Light,
6. Existence, and
7. Thought.

Energetically, we are a combination of all seven states. We may not fully understand this in our physical body on this third dimensional plane. However, all of our aspects exist simultaneously, on many dimensional planes. As a result, all energetics are able to be intermingled in the soul level.

"We must respect our mouths, as we are conscious of what we say, only when we comprehend what we say. When we don't understand what we say, what comes out of our mouths can be misinterpreted by the ears of others, in different ways. When we hold it to intent, it is never misinterpreted." Wise words from creation!

People cannot mistake your intent in words, if you have faith in what you are saying. You become transparent immediately if you don't believe in what you are saying or if you choose to express untruths in your personal space. Integrity is paramount if you want truth and light in your life. Manipulating words costs integrity, but expression of truth in feelings really enables others to find their alignment with you and your credibility is not questionable. You will find others having faith in your advice and general integrity, easily, if you always speak from your heart and light.

DIMENSIONAL PLANES

There are seven dimensional planes of existence, which intermingle with our environment of Earth.

- *The first dimensional plane* holds the rocks, earth, and crystals.
- *The second dimensional plane* holds all plant life, herbs, and the devic realm (fairies, earth spirits, et cetera).
- *The third dimensional plane* is the earth, our space-time continuum, how we see our reality as humans upon the earth plane.
- *The fourth dimensional plane* holds the spirit world, discarnate beings, guides, et cetera.
- *The fifth dimensional plane* holds the angels, archangels, and ascended masters.
- *The sixth dimensional plane* holds the tones, colour laws, and laws of the universe, which hold all the workings together.
- *The seventh dimensional plane* is "the creation plane," as Creator described it to me.

Creator said, "The seven dimensional planes are not separate planes. They are separate states as such. As separate states, they coexist in all aspects simultaneously."

HOW TO HEAL WITH THE CREATOR

Our Creator says, "There is no separation between heaven and earth. It all coexists in the same space. All of us are God, in God, with God, around God, and of God. We need only pray with highest intent to be connected to the creator, and all energetics in our wisdom are activated simultaneously to enable us to be activated consciously with the creative force; that is us, as well as is inspiration". I interpret from this quote from Creator that the last statement "that is us as well as inspiration" means that we have available to us all that we can hope to find already, in a graceful state of connection which inspires us to be our best and greatest self spiritually. We exist in a state of all that is.

It is quotes like those above that I find so inspiring in my personal interactions with the creative force. It is a special place for me when I interact with this level of wisdom and light. I feel truly blessed and on track to my own spirituality. I find advice in the interactions and conversations I have with God. It is my hope that you will also be facilitated to have faith in your own interactions with our Creator and that you can facilitate this with personal faith and empowerment directly, without the need for an interpretive messenger. This is the aim of my workshops: Personal Empowerment in Connection to That which Created You.

Channelled from the Creator:

"Upon the Earth plane at this time there are many energies of negativity roaming. It is not for you to worry of these things for they are being countered of love and light."

ENLIGHTENMENT

Creator says, "Enlightenment ensues as it becomes the same possibility as light refracting inside a crystal."

Within a faceted crystal, light will enter and fragment into the appropriate colour spectrum, as it does in the cellular structure of the water molecules.

There is no ability of light to exist in dark. Therefore, all dark forms will try to repel the light from them. If you make all dark forms penetrable by light, they are unable to defend themselves and they disappear.

The idea of *enlightenment* is, in actual fact, the idea of *light*ening the cellular structure of the body, as well as the auric fields and aspects of the person. The continual light beams reflect and refract from all facets of the prism and will continue unless there is blockage. Blockage can, in turn, be penetrated by persistent light and therefore must no longer exist.

When love and light are beamed into a space, dense energy, or anything that has held a residue that is not of unconditional love, is inhibited from vibrating at a frequency other than the appropriate frequency of light and therefore cannot survive. Concisely put, light will dispel darkness, whether it is dis-ease, energy blockage, or a thought form belonging to another being or emotion.

As you evolve and become an "enlightened being," there is more light in your body. Therefore, you are simply less able to hold the negative thought forms that would "disenlighten" you and make you into a being not vibrating at the pure love of Buddha, Jesus, and other beings who are considered "enlightened masters."

To recap, if you are not holding the negative emotions or dis-eases, for example, thought forms of anger and hatred, you become free, are in balance, and *enlightened*. Your frequency is lightening; that is why you are ascending. *Enlightenment . . .* You vibrate less densely, higher, and lighter!

THE INCARNATIONAL STAR

The *incarnational star* is a portal space existing within the body. It exists energetically one inch above the navel and one inch inside the body, approximately. This is the energetic point of inception of the soul energy into the physical body in the third dimensional plane, as the energy comes to the body at conception or soul entry.

As beings, we travel as souls into the foetus during pregnancy. This can happen anywhere from conception to soon before birth, although most souls enter the body between two to five months of gestation. The incarnational star is the entryway for this process.

During my workshop, I guide you to travel through this portal space in meditation in a safe and gentle manner, whilst connected to Creator. You can gain knowledge and experience the spiritual dimension that exists in the time between lifetimes, prior to your own conception. From this place, you can learn about your spiritual intentions and aims in this lifetime.

Please note, you will only be given the information that is safe and necessary for your evolution by spirit, so no overwhelm is possible. The universe only ever has unconditional love and peace as its intentions.

LAUGHTER AND SPIRITUALITY

Don't be surprised if you find yourself laughing during any connection process with creation or during any of these meditations, as well as finding awareness. Spirit is always in favour of a good laugh, I have found.

Creator spoke with me during one of my "question-and-answer" sessions where I ask Creator about things I want to have explained. Creator informed me that, to the beings of light, laughter has been described, along with love, as the most powerful force in the Universal Plan for Peace. Humans are capable of great love and laughter. If you consider it, you cannot commit any act of aggression and be truly laughing at the same time, in love. It isn't possible. Therefore, entertaining laughter is a genuine gift to peace and love on this planet.

When I am doing healing work, I often find Creator showing me funny pictures, which are deliberately placed to lighten the atmosphere and make me amused. The client always benefits from the relay of information, and the healing session becomes one of fun and laughter. Isn't that a great aim of our creation—to find love, peace, and laughter in all our interactions? Why not with God then?

We can have a distorted view of spiritual interaction if we place any guilt or punishment paradigms in our consciousness. We don't have any requirement, expected by God, other than to have love and joy in our lives. A truthful conscience is such an important part of living a good life and doing good work. We may forget to include laughter and joy for ourselves, and others, as a normal paradigm of our interactions. One of the things often said to me by clients, who repeatedly come for healing, is how good they feel after interacting with me and Creator. They often comment that this was unexpected because they judge themselves or have been judged or taught that they won't measure up or perhaps will be judged severely by God. They find forgiveness and explanation. God said to me, "Why would I need to punish anyone when they are so good at doing it themselves?" Is this a key to our humanity? Are we self-regulators even of our own punishments?

Yes, I believe we often are. If we create our reality, then surely we must also create a potential for our own punishments or guilt, if we feel the need to attract them. This is an open statement obviously, because we are not always responsible, directly, for all interactions with the free will of others we encounter. However, in the broader sense, we attract energy according to our belief systems, so the broader set-up can assume qualities of our own making.

TALKING AND INTERACTING WITH ANIMALS

Well, for those of us who have been lucky enough to have an animal live with us, the experience can be both gentle and demanding, nurturing and offensive. Cleaning up poo and other such things can be a challenge to the house-proud, and general brushing and caring routines get in the way of a social get-together occasionally. I find that in general, our pets are very forgiving of our misdemeanours . . . well, I hope we are of theirs too. They are usually pretty loyal, especially dogs. Cats tend to think you are supposed to look after them, thank you very much, and that is just the way it is! Usually, they act a little haughty if you disturb their routine and don't like sharing too much. They stay on the couch, sofa, bed, or in front of the hearth and look pretty darn good most of the time. Then they snuggle and want to be played with, and we fall in love with their furry softness all over again. Some cats are mischievous, some playful. There is a difference!

All species have a character-specific trait and a "big kahuna" energetic, which is like the head of the species. I have, more than once, removed an impending beehive invasion by speaking and negotiating with the energy in charge of the hive. I have explained that they needed to move on to another environment and not settle in my space. Just last month, I had such an experience and held a conversation with the being in charge.

I explained it just wasn't appropriate to inhabit my roof and that we, as humans, found that threatening. I asked if they could move on into the vacant bush block next to my home, or elsewhere, where there could be undisturbed trees awaiting them and the threat of man would be less intrusive. I was joyfully surprised to find the swarm move out of the eaves within five to ten minutes. The bees have not been seen since. I did not have to resort to the explanation that pest fumigators may have had to be called in if they weren't cooperative. Why? Because there was nothing other than a polite agenda coming my way. You see, we are imposing on their natural environment with our structures, and so they did not understand the significance of their inconvenience to us. Our structures get in the way of naturally flowing air currents of the land design.

Once I had explained my predicament, they were fine about moving on. I much prefer this approach.

I have had many funny experiences in connection with animals. I remember how I learned to speak with them in this way. I was once asked by telephone one morning to look at a client's horse, using distant perception or healing. This was at least ten years ago, and I remember being more than daunted by the idea. I wondered if I could scan or read an animal and receive information that would satisfy my client. So I connected to Creator's energy and asked what to do. I was directed to speak with the higher self of the animal concerned and told that it did not have to be onsite with us for me to do this. Lucky, as a draught horse in the lounge isn't my idea of fun!

So I said to the client that I would have a go and asked what she was actually after. She informed me that the horse was lying down at the foot of the paddock and refusing to get up. Apparently, she was refusing regular feed, appeared sulky, and wasn't listening or cooperating as she usually did. I asked if they knew of any circumstances that might have contributed to this injury. I was informed they did not but that the horse did have "a difficult temperament on occasion."

Well, I had the funniest conversation with this wonderful animal. However, it wasn't at all what I expected. I am blessed with the gift of auric sense. That is, I hear everything in words. Those who know me personally know I like to converse, so I can't really be surprised as to why that would be! God likes a chat too!

I connected to the higher self of the animal and was dumbstruck to hear a whiney, neurotic, highly pitched voice speaking at full speed and complaining about her lot! I did not expect that, I can assure you. Apparently, she was annoyed . . . yes, really annoyed . . . that her owner's daughter had not been visiting her lately. As a result, she was missing out on her daily molasses, thereby leading to the proverbial sulking hissy-fit, which I was privileged to witness.

The horse said, "I am refusing to be cooperative because I am not appreciated, and therefore if they do not give me more attention, I am lying in the paddock and will remain there until they do."

You can imagine that to be having this conversation in my mind with a horse, out of the blue, isn't what I expected. In addition, I did think my client might think I was a little insane if I expressed the above. However, when I relayed, tactfully, what I had been told, the lady burst into laughter and confirmed that she believed what I was saying. She described the horse "as quite neurotic at times," prone to seeking attention, and said that her daughter had in fact been away for some days and the horse had, consequently, missed her molasses, which was the treat usually brought by her daughter.

The feedback given led to a successful conclusion to this problem. The client delivered molasses to the horse that day. The horse got up, and the owner thought she could see a smile from her draught horse, who seemed very pleased to be again getting extra attention.

This interaction led me to wanting to explore animal communication more fully. I had two cats with whom I then commenced regular healings and chats about mundane things, like how they felt they were treated at home and whether they needed anything. The feedback was to buy a more expensive cat food brand, please, and not to forget to empty the litter tray.

On a holiday a few years ago, I visited a popular nature park in Queensland, Australia. It is full of different species and became my playground. Whilst my teenage children went on the fairground rides, I spent a lovely day in the koala and bird sanctuary, chatting away like mad with everything I could. I thought I could experiment with seeing if different species had a common personality or if individuals within the species had different personalities, like we do. Well, I can tell you that turtles have different personalities! The two with whom I spoke did at least.

I was taking a paddle-boat ride, which runs slowly and quietly in a lagoon in the nature reserve area of this fun park. In the lagoon, there were turtles, eels, various species of fish, and I assume platypus too, although I did not see any that day. Floating alongside the boat were two turtles, approximately a metre apart. One looked very docile, with slow and languid stretching movements of its green limbs. The other turtle was rapidly darting about in the reeds on the top of the water, checking out the crowd who were checking out the turtles! He seemed to have a completely disparate attitude to the other, so I was immediately attracted to experiment with some conversation with them both. My goal was to see if they felt, or experienced, differently to me.

Again, as I am blessed with conversation in words, I was treated to some statements in language. I assume this comes into my mind in a frequency of energy that my mind interprets and then puts into words. I think I must assess the nuances of the frequency, which is also an assessment of personality. All I know is that when I hear the conversation, it verbalises, even with an accent! Really! It is very funny, and I am sure, as I chuckled, the other holidaymakers on the boat moved a little away from the odd lady sitting on the floor intently staring at the turtles, with some weird expressions and odd giggles. Well, you possibly would!

I can only provide my replay of the conversation, but it gives you the gist.

Conversation in thoughts projected via connecting to the higher self of the turtle, using the connection to Creator process, as follows:

Me to slow Turtle Number One: "Hallo. What are you doing?"
Turtle Number One in a drawling voice reminiscent of the groovy turtle on the children's movie
    Finding Nemo: "Uuur . . . nothing much, just hanging around."
Me: "Oh, you sound very slow and cruisey."
Turtle Number one: "Uur, yeah."
Me: "Can you tell me anything about yourself?"
Turtle Number One: "I like swimming. It is hot here. Who are you?"
Me: "I am just curious because I wondered what life is like for you."
Turtle Number One: "Oh yeah, good."

He then seemed disinterested in continuing the conversation further and just cruised about in basically the same place, near the boat for the slow process of circumnavigating the lagoon. He seemed happy just to hang around close to the people.

Me to Turtle Number Two: "Hallo. How are you?"

Turtle Number Two in a clipped accent reminiscent of Oxford English replied: "Well, how would you be if you had to be confined to this?"

Me: "Oh you speak very differently to that other turtle over there."

I then signified the turtle I was referring to with my intent.

Turtle Number Two: "Yes, well, he is not very intelligent, is he? What would you expect?"

Me: "I am really surprised you are so different to him; I thought you may be similar as turtles."

Turtle Number Two: "Well, there is no accounting for taste, is there?"

At this point, I thanked him. He said, "Good-bye," and that was the end of that interaction.

I would suspect you may be sceptical at this point, but I assure you that if you learn how to interact with animals as many others have done on my classes, you will actually see that this is not unusual. It really is possible to have animal communication. Two of my students are, in fact, veterinarians. Both have commented on how valuable the skill has become in diagnosis, as each has been able to interact with the animal and ask specifically about symptoms and about its pain, et cetera. Apparently, it is now not uncommon practice for them to consult and advise the owners, as the animals can manifest the disease of their owners too.

I have had occasion to speak with ill animals prior to their passing over. It is a great skill, and it is a comfort to the pet owners to be able to know for sure what is happening with their animal. We often do become as close to our pets as children. Of course, when faced with difficult decisions like whether to have an animal euthanized when injured or in disease which has become serious, we want to be fully informed and ethical in our decision-making process, on behalf of these beings.

I will never forget the majesty and sacredness of an interaction I had with two black parrots sitting in the bird enclosure that day at the nature park. They were a breeding pair, male and female, sitting next to each other high on a perch made from a dead tree branch. They were silently sitting, surrounded by koalas on perches, and looking at the crowd walking along pathways at the foot of the enclosure. The path, at one point, inclined to the roof. This was where I was standing, nearing the top of the netting directly to the right of them and about six metres away.

I wanted to connect to Creator and speak to them. So, as you do, I put on my sunglasses so everyone didn't think I was a crazy person standing there with my eyes closed and fluttering (as the eyelids often do this when you are in the theta brainwave).

When connected, I spoke to the male parrot and had a brief and respectful conversation. I finished, grounded myself, and opened my eyes to look at the parrot. The next thing that happened had me spellbound. The male parrot was staring directly at me, making eye contact. He nudged his mate, to his left side, who was facing away from me. She turned and also stared directly at me.

They were both looking directly at me, and both nodded their heads in a joint acknowledgement, simultaneously. I was so amazingly moved by the grace and majesty of these royal birds, which stand about half a metre tall. It was something so touching, to connect in a real way with the spirit of these wonderful beings.

Thank you for listening. My eyes get teary as I write this. It was an occasion you probably only get once when you really need the confirmation and you are truly in a respectful place with Mother Nature and her creatures.

KNOW YOUR GUIDANCE TEAM

They may turn up at any time in your life. During my Abundance workshop, participants often received direct personal advice whilst exploring the section of this workshop which concentrated on understanding of the soul's true purpose and desire.

So, what is a guidance team? We each have a guardian angel who is allocated to us at our birth and who will remain with us for the entirety of this lifetime. You get a new one each lifetime usually.

In addition to our official guardian angel, we also have a team of players who assist our journey. They may be for different reasons, styles, times, and places. For example, you can have one guide who may help you with family, one for work, one for a specific theme of occupation, and one for play. You may have a chorus of angels, be a light worker needing specific guided advice on a theme for greater good work, and find yourself in the middle of a soul purpose revelation. You may find yourself truly empowered and that you have a team assisting the revelations you are about to encounter.

You may have Earth sprites like elves, divas, fairies, and tree dwellers of high resonance, who work with the Earth paradigms.

It often depends on what your theme of interest is at the time. They may move in and out. So don't think it queer if you see a fairy or an elf. It isn't all that unusual!

However, we all want to contact our major guidance players, so you may also see some of the ascended masters or archangels along for the day.

You won't be allocated a personal ascended master within your own guidance team. You may find the master's resonance present, assisting you with whatever area you are working on at the time that you view your guidance team. Sometimes, if you feel you need specific protection, you may see Archangel Michael working with you and the Earth of your land or your children and family members being heralded into a safe haven.

Jesus and Mary will turn up if needed. So may Kwan Yin and Lao Tsu or any of the beings of the etheric, who are here to work with Creator's specific plan for our planet and its beings. That is, after all, what happens if you pray! It is no different to orthodox religion where you may ask for guidance or pray to a specific angel. You are doing the same and just connecting in a very conscious way to interact for feedback and advice. Don't feel you are violating any traditional church teachings by asking to speak to your angels. I think that is considered the norm. Well, that is how I interpret it anyway. It is a wonderful and inspiring place to play!

Your guides often change when you do a major shift. Shifts will become easier once you have these tools.

Often, you will receive your guidance via clues, coincidences, and occurrences in your life that have an impact upon you. As you become practiced at reaching the Creator or requesting specific information, you will be able to converse directly with Source. You may develop visions containing pictures, interact in conversation, or just perceive the "knowing" that comes with direct contact with spirit.

Would you like to experiment with speaking directly with your own guidance team? You may try the exercise here and enjoy the practice.

You can ask to be connected to your guardian angels and guides for specific guidance at any time.

Firstly, you follow the connection process, as shown to you earlier in this book.

Once connected, you hold the intent to speak and interact with your own guidance team, as sent by the Creator, in truth, light, and unconditional love.

Imagine yourself floating in the ethers and them approaching your space, to interact with you in love and light. Enjoy the practice.

Once you have made the connection, you can ask any questions you choose. You will become, with practice, very good at this interaction. We are all born with this gift in place. It is not something you are trying to attain. It is, rather, something about which you are unblocking the fog! They are already there just waiting for you to wake up and have a chat. Be aware not to give yourself any achievement anxiety in the process.

Often, people don't see very much the first time. You can ask Creator to zoom in and out like a camera, to explain in symbols or words, in order to provide clarity. Just play, and don't take yourself too seriously. Let the information and knowledge just glide into your space. That way, you won't be overwhelmed by the thought of interacting with these major players of the etheric and will allow them to nurture you with information.

When you think you have interacted enough and gleaned the information or experience you wanted, just imagine yourself returning to your body, thanking them for the interaction before you go. Imagine yourself surrounded by Creator's blue light on your way back into your body, and ground yourself again. This is the same process as previously described.

Don't forget to write down anything you received immediately, as you may well forget it otherwise. This tends to happen when you come back into the beta brainwave of consciousness from the theta brainwave, which is just like dreaming. Do you remember everything about your dreams for long? That is what I mean!

One of the things I am often asked is whether we could be bothering our angels if we keep asking for assistance. Don't forget that your angels are there waiting for you to contact them or ask for their assistance every day. It is OK to ask. You won't be taking up their time unduly. They are there just for *you*. It would be frustrating to be hanging around waiting for a shift for work and find you are not rostered on most days, don't you think? Luckily, angels don't have performance anxiety or feel neglected. However, I am sure they will be more than willing to be present, when requested, for some personal time with you. Remember to have fun with them. All beings like to feel happy and appreciated, so say thank you. In all things, services provided come unconditionally in spirit.

Information about the Skills I Teach

In the next few pages, I show you what was in my workshops, which are now able to be transferred to one-on-one mentoring sessions as appropriate and may draw on any one of the subsequent pages of learning. The information has been left unrevised in this book as a guide to show you what may be possible if you choose this pathway and Creator says it is appropriate for you to work with me in this way. It is something you may consider.

WHAT WAS IN MY STAGE-1 WORKSHOP?

How to Connect to That which Created You—
Experiential Connection Workshop

This two-day workshop is designed to follow up from what you have already read. It is useful for both beginners who have never experimented with their connection to Creator yet and also the more advanced. In all things, you take from it whatever you are ready to assimilate; therefore, you can enjoy connection at your own pace.

In life, we often feel we have to achieve to be acceptable. One of the things we are most fearful of is being judged, failing, or looking foolish.

In these workshops, there is no competition. It is not meant to be an achievement-oriented seminar. What I encourage is participation, having a go, being yourself, having a lot of fun, and laughing. These are general principles for a fulfilling life experience. In my many years of teaching, the most prevalent thing I have witnessed in participants is a real desire to experience their own empowerment but a great fear of it as well. Perhaps, we could say we most often experience a fear of achievement, not necessarily performance. What if we don't measure up to another? Really, that should not be the important thing in our lives. The mere act of indulging that thinking pattern will hold us back from true appreciation of ourselves, the moment, and the little gems of our interactions.

I place no importance on comparisons but only on awareness of self in your connection to the universe. You deserve time and appreciation purely for being yourself and existing. Coming to a seminar should not be daunting but exciting. That is why my workshops and now working parties are full of fun and laughter. They contain experiential exercises, so you can practice and feel competent in the techniques you have been taught. Theory is only of so much benefit in any learning, but practical experience is a solid and concrete teacher, whose lessons we tend to remember. It makes us feel enticed to participate and learn . . . without stress.

In my stage-1 workshop, I introduce participants to the process of connection to Creator, talking much more about frequency and the importance of words. We learn to connect and to interact directly with that creative force, asking questions that we personally need to have answered to assist us on our path. We learn how to do energetic healing on ourselves and others in a gentle format whilst connected to Creator. Enticingly, we also learn to connect to crystals, interacting with them via the creative force and having a crystal perform a healing on us!

We experience deep meditations:

a) travelling to meet God
b) travelling into the heart
c) travelling into Gaia (Mother Earth) and the consciousness of Gaia
d) travelling through the portal of the incarnational star into the time between lifetimes

In my life, there are music and song. Come and experience the joyfulness of connection. You may experience personal connection to the place of all there is . . . an entertaining and new awareness of personal spirituality.

WHAT WAS IN MY STAGE-2 WORKSHOP?

Gaining Competence in Your Connection and Healing

During the course of the learnings from this workshop, you may very well surprise yourself with your competence and grace. After having completed the stage-1 workshop or beginners' mentoring day, you can now play and cement your previously learned skills. We indulge ourselves in more advanced conversations with God, with more information being delivered about the process. Another great aspect of this workshop is that you receive more information about healings, enabling you to advance in your knowledge.

Have you ever wanted to converse with animals or even heal them? During this wonderful workshop, via our connection with Creator, we learned to speak and interact with animals. Any animal may be contacted. All beings have a need for nurturing and assistance at some time in their lives. This is where you can perform wonderful connections and healings with the higher self of an animal. You can effect a physical healing on your own animals by requesting their permission and acting alongside Creator to witness their improved condition. It is very rewarding having a conversation with another species. Have you ever considered that as a possibility?

Well, it is actually quite simple to do. Once you have established connection with the creature at whom you are directing your intent, you may ask questions, learn, and experience life from its point of view. Interacting directly with the personality of the animal enables you to be empathetic to its plight or condition and also to understand this planet from the perspective of another of God's creatures.

Often, whilst speaking with animals, I find myself humbled by their grace or struck by the awesomeness of their personal journeys. This is an absolutely wonderful skill to possess. I strongly recommend that, if you are intrigued or involved with animals in any aspect of your life, you allow yourself to benefit from the facility of conversation with them and the capacity to perform healings where acceptable.

Soul / body communication: In your body, you communicate with spirit via the connection point of the pineal gland, which connects to the soul star and works with it. The pineal gland and incarnational star are linked as one, in the energetic of aligning the physical body to the soul's true purpose.

A few years ago, in one of my workshops, I had a participant, an older man, whom I considered extremely enlightened and gentle in the ways of Zen. He had spent five years in solitary contemplation in China, in a monastery, and was a practicing master of Qi Gong. He informed me that the old masters work for many years to achieve alignment of the soul meridian. They are aware of its existence and perform diligent, daily practice to work toward it and then to keep it attuned. Apparently, it can take up to five years of effort to achieve this. During my workshop, you will receive this in an amazing and fulfilling attunement process. Creator has given me the understanding of performing this process as an energetic attunement, which I have now been doing for eight years with great success. I receive consistently wonderful feedback from participants, who state they have achieved a sense of balance and cognizance of their soul, which they had not previously experienced.

Meditations are most fulfilling. We look at why we are here and our soul's purpose and desire.

We will also be discussing water! Yes, there is new information about water, its personal space on this planet, and what we can achieve with new knowledge about this amazing substance and its consciousness and constant capacity for flow.

I plan to produce a new book about this amazing substance, containing understanding channelled from creation in their desire to provide information to us about this wonderful being.

WHAT WAS IN MY STAGE-3 ABUNDANCE WORKSHOP?

Increasing One's Abundance whilst Connected to the Universe

Abundance! Yes, we all want to understand how to be more fulfilled and abundant in our lives. This workshop requires only the completion of the stage 1 introductory workshop in order to participate.

Intensive understanding of your personal journey is the aim here. We explore issues that block your personal understanding of abundance in your life. You will be shown how to unblock future pathways for progression in your life and given guidance for inner well-being. We also spend time exploring the blocks you may have, those you have instituted yourself that block your personal journey and connection.

This is one for self-discovery.

You will be shown how to muscle test so you can explore your subconscious core belief systems. The subconscious mind is actually storing your unconscious beliefs, not the conscious mind!

You will be shown how to check yourself for allergies, via the kinesiology technique known as muscle testing, and shown how to ask the body what suits you.

WHAT ARE MY STAGE-4 TRAVEL WORKING PARTIES ALL ABOUT?

I still conduct these working parties. When God calls . . . we come a-runnin'!

Actually, these workshops will be by invitation from Creator, to those in the network who have completed at least stage 1 of my workshops or personal mentoring. When the Earth needs us, we go where we are needed, supplying our healing talents to the focus Creator provides, onsite. Often, we can work distantly when performing Earth healing, but occasionally, we need to be present with the Earth's energy onsite. If that happens, I will give you a call and ask you if you are interested. Come and join the network!

WHAT WAS IN MY STAGE-5 WORKSHOP?

This was a workshop to assist you in progressing from your currently acquired knowledge of self, in this lifetime, into the revelations of other lifetimes.

As a being of multifactorial input, you exist on many levels of beingness. As a soul, you interact with creation in many ways. One of our intentions on this planet is to acquire knowledge of our many selves. If you believe in reincarnation, you understand the principles of acquiring experience, lifetime after lifetime. The principle intent is to become a fully enlightened being, sitting alongside Creator fully ascended and of a high experience base, enabling you to understand all that exists.

That is the aim of the soul at its inception. We spend our lives reexploring our possibilities and heart's desires and goals, acquiring perceptiveness, and specialising in the factors of our soul's mastership. We have talents and belong to councils as a soul who specialises in aspects based on the theme to which our soul intention belongs. That is, we may be souls invested in caring for Gaia or perhaps charity and children, light work, et cetera.

This workshop was designed to help you explore yourself on past-life or perhaps future-existence levels. We explore interconnections with other souls and learn how to gain clearance and healing if we have difficulties connected to other lifetimes and perceptions from those lifetimes. We learn how to clear pathways to others with whom we have difficulties. We develop understanding of ourselves in our *now* and explore why we have come again. We are able to clear and heal incongruities in our feelings and behaviour patterns. On occasion it is possible to experience feelings of being compelled in our behaviours in our now and to experience a sense of deja vu or dischord. We may wonder why this is happening when there seems to be no logical basis for these feelings, patterns and behaviours. They can be imprinted behaviours which have been carried from one lifetime to another to be resolved. This is an explorative and fun workshop. You can heal past hurts and gain insight all at the same time. Wonderful work! I offer this learning in personal mentoring days now also.

BLESSINGS AND GRATITUDE

Each day can be filled with wonder. Often, it is in the housework and washing up! Learning to appreciate and place love in the little things is an art form worth cultivating.

This is an excerpt from my first edition of this book.

Living with teenage boys can be a challenge, but I also see the grace in their athleticism, the fun in their mischief, the appreciation of and wonder at the world of science. I have been known to become frustrated and enraged about the state of the kitchen benches and the raided fridge; packets discarded right next to the bin. I wonder that they don't notice the washing on the bathroom floor. However, if I need a helping hand they come and help me because, they tell me, they appreciate and love me. They respect my efforts and I find that very supportive. My children have seen me working hard to support them as a single mum. Now that I have found my soul partner they see us as a family unit, which is comforting. My youngest child is of primary-school age and needs extra care and play time. My eldest child is married and she is an excellent mother, and a true friend. She and her husband have blessed this world with four gorgeous children. I visit them as often as time, and our schedules, permit. My heart sings when I hear the little ones call me Oma (Dutch for grandmother). It can be a struggle to work, be a parent and take care of a business, as well as a family. I am, however, eternally grateful for the opportunity to grow and experience via these unique beings. I am taught every day, so I grow every day. That is a blessing.

My home is just that—a home. It's not a pristine showpiece, but a clean and tidy-most-of-the-time home. Built of earth-coloured brick, on almost two acres of land on the top of a hill, it overlooks the southern ocean and beaches, farming land and a small town. Wildlife and birds abound on my property because I have left it as close to its natural landscape as possible, with plentiful trees and havens for the animals. Yes, the lawn gets mowed and the flowers tended, the garden beds blessed and the divas (earth spirits) informed prior to any garden activity. This is so they can prepare themselves and their habitat for what is to come from my space.

A month ago, I held a working party at my home, to perform some greater good work with a group of special friends who have done this work with me over the last few years. Two of the men had flown in from Queensland and one of the ladies from an island north of Darwin in the Northern Territory. One travelled from Melbourne, and the rest were locals from Tasmania. We spent days doing healing work, as asked by Creator, on topics like pollution, whales, child health, and communication on the planet. Just prior to the commencement of the working party, there were terrific storms throughout the region with winds reaching 120 kilometres per hour. Consequently, some trees came down in the winds and we had much garden cleanup to do. A tree branch was overhanging my deck, so my friends took some time out to assist with its removal. However, unlike the usual tree-lopping event, ours went like this:

How many people does it take to lop a tree branch?—Nine!

One man . . . using a chainsaw,

One man . . . in a car with rope tensioning the limb away from the house,

One man . . . assisting with tie up and clearing the vicinity,

Six women allocated energetic healing jobs, whilst apparently watching,

First woman . . . healing and supporting the tree during the operation of removing its limb with the chainsaw,

Second woman . . . supporting safety for the chainsaw operator,

Third woman . . . supporting safety for the other two men performing the work,

Fourth woman . . . clearing the air of the extreme sound of the chainsaw so the birds and animals would not be upset,

Fifth woman . . . healing animals and creatures in the vicinity who found the process upsetting

Sixth woman . . . informing and blessing the divas, whilst the operation was happening on the land. This was done whilst laughing her head off and blessing in grace for the joy of these friends . . . holding the energy of light for her abundance! *Me*!

A day before I spent the day writing to conclude this book, my darling partner was outside on the ride-on lawnmower, struggling a little with the overgrowth on the front paddock. In our region, we have had, for the first season in many seasons, plentiful rain. We have been doing conscious Earth healing work to assist the weather phenomenon in our region. It seems to be working, although some might say it is an effect of global warming. I tend to the feeling that it is in fact some form of resolve. Our area has been in drought for some time and the farmers severely challenged, having to cull stock last year as there was no feed, with dams almost empty and creek beds running dry.

To be blessed with plentiful, lush, verdant, and healthy grass to mow, and the colour to behold is an absolute treat for us, and we are grateful. Our house is serviced only by water tanks, so we really don't have sufficient supply to water the garden. I have planted drought-hardy shrubs and trees. Nevertheless, my land is always healthy, with trees self-sowing everywhere. Even in extremely dry conditions, my land seems better off compared to the neighbourhood, often having plentiful growth. This is due to the blessings and healings I do daily on my land, trees, divas, and animals, including the birds that nest here and those that pass overhead. They all get nurturing.

My partner had done a good deal of the lawn mowing when he came inside, about dinnertime, with a huge smile on his face. He asked me if I had finished yet, and when I said, "Almost," he said, "Me too, except I got to make you a present." I was wondering how he had managed that whilst being on the recently acquired, hot-red ride-on mower that he loves. He grinned and said, "Well, I was bopping away with my iPod on to 'Sisters Are Doin' It for Themselves,' by Aretha Franklin and Annie Lennox, and feeling so good that I got inspired to make a crop circle." And there was his present . . . a huge love heart with a cupid arrow in it, carefully mowed into the front paddock! His hug and the "I so love you, darling," were just the most moving affirmation of our relationship that I wanted to hear and feel.

Now for my updated life in January 2013.

My husband, my youngest child, and I moved to Port Macquarie in New South Wales, Australia, a year ago. We have a suburban house full of love and joy. My eldest son moved to a warmer climate seven hours' drive north of us. My daughter and family and my second son stayed in Tasmania, and as adults, all three have their own homes and lives now. That is a huge wrench for any mum, but we are so very close in our hearts and visit each other whenever we are able. I recently had a houseful (a much smaller house than before) of eleven people having early Christmas . . . All my children, my son-in-law, and four grandchildren plus my husband and I all making merry woopee and noise, laughter, and silly putty so to speak. We put up the Christmas tree, loved each other, played the piano and guitar, shared our life stories, and went kayaking on the local river. My new home is blessed with rain forest five minutes one side, the ocean five minutes the other side, and a river just north. This is the sea change aspect of life where you take stock, scale down, and love and laugh in joy with God and creation. I wish you that in your life. It is well worth the integrity it takes to uphold all your values and to empower yourself without fear as you change direction.

Abundance always goes with flow!

Now you see how blessings and gratitude fulfil us.

Attract to you that which you deserve.
Be what you know you are in your heart.
Never give up hope of a bright and light future.
You are what you think, so think with optimism.
Explore that which makes your heart sing.
Try until it gets easier; don't give up.
Laugh, and be heartily surprised at your every day.
Respect, love, and light the way in your creation with our Creator.

Then you will always keep your light burning bright!

Love, light, and blessings in all ways,

Katherine Bright